Title: What you believe ... Happens! / Marc Ducasse (English Translation)

Name: Ducasse, Marc, 1955- author.

Identifier: ISBN 978-2-9816427-3-8

Cover infographic and layout: Marc Ducasse

Linguistic translation from french Novel - Ce que tu crois... Devient! - : Emily Hoopkins

Publisher: Marc Ducasse

Telephone.: 514 360-6096

Email: contact@marcducasse. com

Website: www. marcducasse. com

ISBN paper version: 978-2-9816427-7-6

ISBN digital epdf version: 978-2-9816427-8-3

ISBN digital epub version: 978-2-9816427-4-5

Legal Deposit:

National Library of Québec

Library and Archives Canada

© 2020 Marc Ducasse

What You Believe...
Becomes!

Introduction

After the success of his first novel, (*Even Flies Follow the Seasons*) Marc Ducasse returns to explore in his own way the meaning of life through his characters, all of whom are as surprising as they are crazy, in order to help readers become conscious of their ability to create the lives they desire and discover their own ways to personal happiness.

Summary

What you believe... Becomes! Makes us aware of the power we all have to change our lives.

To be able to understand our successes and our failures, without looking outside ourselves to find who is to blame, is simpler than we think, and is the goal of this book.

Jack (the man who has everything, and who is on the verge of losing everything) with the help of Bruno (the itinerant who seems to know a lot more than he seems) as well as several others, will discover what he no longer understands. One after another, each person will help him little by little to find meaning in life.

A story that may resemble your own; though told in a a different way, from a different situation or from a different point of view, it might not be too different from yours.

We can all change and become what we want if we get to know ourselves enough.

This novel brings us, slowly, towards the discovery which is simply... ourselves.

Happy Reading,
Marc Ducasse :)

The Journey

<u>The Note</u>

Don't worry,
I'm fine despite the circumstances. I need to find myself. I ask you to not try to look for me. Trust me. I will keep you posted. I made sure that you and the children would not want for anything.
I love you... xxx

<u>**There**</u>

- Here...
- Thank you!

The two men stood side by side, shivering. The incessant rain and bad weather had brought the two strangers together after the destruction of their respective shelters.

The guy looked at the piece of bread he had just received, not taking a bite, when he heard:

- You can eat it, you know. It's for you, said the man who had given it to him.
- I know, but...
- What?
- I feel like I'm taking the little you have, he said, looking at the dilapidated state of the place where they found themselves, and...
- Don't worry, you can't take much from me. And as far as that goes, the man continued, pointing to the piece of bread, I've already eaten some and I was keeping it just in case, and now, the "in case" is you.
- Thanks again, said the guy, taking a bite. My name is Jack, and you?
- Bruno.

The two homeless men were looking at each other, one feeling at home, the other not.

<u>**The Opposite**</u>

- Have you been living like this for a long time?

Bruno, who was busy hanging his clothes over a block of cement to dry them, now that the bad weather had passed, turned around.
- You should do the same, he said, ignoring the question while gesturing to the clothes. You might get a skin condition if you stay in wet clothes.
- I thought I would do it when you were done.
- Don't be shy for me. There is room for everyone.
- Very well, replied Jack, following the man's example and beginning to undress.
- You'll see, it dries very quickly on cement.
- Let me repeat my question, said Jack, drawing closer, have you been living on the street for a long time?
- Longer than you, if you judge by your *clean-cut haircut,* and your not very worn clothes. It's been over a week since I've seen you around.
- ...
- What about you? asked Bruno, seeing that Jack said nothing.
- Less time than you, if you judge by your New-wave-shaved-on-the-side long-time-no-cut haircut, and your worn-out clothes.

Bruno smiled at the reply and continued:

- It's kind of strange that we've crossed paths in such circumstances, don't you think?
- Do you believe in coincidences? asked Jack in reply.
- Absolutely not, answered Bruno, and you?
- I don't know... I really don't know anymore.
- What do you mean?

- I always thought I knew everything, but now...
- And how is that connected to coincidence?
- I always believed that it was I who established everything that happened in my life and that coincidence had nothing to do with it, but now I'm beginning to doubt.
- And why is that?
- Because I've seen proof to the contrary.
- Be more specific, urged Bruno, intrigued.
- Things happened in my life that I had neither wanted nor planned.
- And you think it was coincidence?
- Exactly, well... I wonder.
- What if it was the opposite? Bruno suggested, as he stopped hanging his clothes to fix him.
- What do you mean?
- That it was you who created what you didn't want, but you just don't know it... yet.

Jack looked at him trying to understand as Bruno began to move away.

<u>Who</u>

- Listen, I'm telling you that you've got it wrong!

After he had finished hanging his clothes, Bruno had headed to the food scrap bins of his favorite restaurant. He rummaged through the piles while listening to Jack, who had followed him.

- I always succeeded in what I started, endured until the end, I always controlled my life and everything that happened in it. So, when you say that I created what I did not want, I do not agree. What I didn't want didn't happen or I quickly got rid of it. I know perfectly how it all works.
- Very well then, replied Bruno still busy with his searching, if you know everything, you have no problems then. I wonder what you are doing here, living on the street, for who knows how long.

Jack stared at his new friend, not knowing what to say.

- We are going to treat ourselves this evening, Bruno commented, showing off his findings. It really is the best restaurant in town.
- I know, replied Jack, looking at the leftovers of the dishes Bruno had in his hands, you should taste it when the meals are fresh, it's even better.
- And how do you know that, Mr. Know-it-all?
- I've been there before, that's how.

Bruno looked at him questioningly before resuming...

- You're going to have to tell me your story, you're getting more and more interesting, he said.
- Not until you have answered my question.

- Which is?

- Why did you say that had I created what I didn't want?

- Because there is nobody else who could do it, except you.

- That is to say?

- Listen, said Bruno, depositing his treasures into his wheeled cart, nobody can create or do something for you. It is only you who have that power. Like me, by the way, and the rest of the planet.

- ...?

- You and me, for example. If you wanted me to do something and I didn't want it, what could you do about it?

- I could force you, use physical force if necessary, there are plenty of ways.

- Okay, but you? Did someone physically force you to do something or did someone do something to you that you didn't want?

- No, of course not.

- And things that you didn't want happened to you anyway?

- Yes...

- Then... who made them, those things you didn't want, if not someone else?

Jack looked at Bruno without saying anything, searching for a satisfactory answer.

- Only you are left... said Bruno, walking away as he pushed his basket.

<u>Accomplices</u>

- Wait...Are you saying that everything that happens to us in life, whether we wanted it or not, is our fault?

Jack struggled to keep up with Bruno, even though Bruno was slowed down by his basket.

- You've got it. You see? It's simple, retorted Bruno, suddenly turning the corner.
- I think you've got to be joking... and would you mind slowing down a bit? I feel like I'm in a grocery cart marathon.
- You're going to have to start training, said Bruno. If you want a good place for the night, you have to get there early.
- First come, first served, right?
- You really are a quick learner.
- Save me a place, please, gasped Jack, stopping to catch his breath.

Bruno continued with a quick step towards the place he coveted, a smile floating across his lips.

Accomplices (Part 2)

-Pretty lucky that you didn't lose a wheel at the speed that you drive, said Jack when he arrived.

Bruno laughed at the reply from his new friend, which triggered Jack's own laughter, which in turn intensified Bruno's laugh. After a good moment of this crazy laughing, the two men stared at each other until Jack admitted:

- It's strange, but I have the feeling that we've known each other for a long time.
  - We may have known each other for a long time...
  - Don't worry, if I knew you before, I would remember.
  - Maybe not...

Jack stared at Bruno, puzzled, before declaring:

- You are something, you know that?
- Really?
- First, you share with me the little you have, you give me your food, you talk to me about creating the life we don't want, and now, you tell me that we may have already met in the past.

Bruno watched Jack in silence; something had changed in his eyes.

- And all that, added Jack, when we've known each other for so short a time.
  - So what?
  - So what? I find it special, that's all.
  - And why is it so special, in your opinion?

- Where I come from, everything is the opposite, explained Jack. Everything is based on competition and adversity, at least in the world in which I have evolved since my birth.

- I understand, replied Bruno.

- And we have nothing for nothing. I have always been taught that there is nothing free in life. So, when you turn up with your beautiful generosity... he whispered, staring at Bruno.

- So?

- So... it makes me ask myself "why?" You who seem to have understood everything, I wonder what you did to live on the street?

- Maybe you are not asking the right questions. Tell me, why did you end up on the street? Why are you here? Why do you seem to no longer understand anything about your life?

Jack, who had turned away while speaking, returned to Bruno.

- You know why you are here? he asked.

- Of course, replied Bruno without hesitation. Probably for the same reason as you.

- Ah yes? Which is?

- And with eyes full of humanity, Bruno replied:

- To find happiness, my friend... that is all!

The Parallel

- Do you live on the street to be happy?

Back at their camp, Jack waited for Bruno, who was busy setting up their shelter for the night, to give him an answer.

- No, that's not what I meant. When I say here, I mean on Earth, in this dimension.
-Listen, if you're here to talk to me about the imaginary world, Heaven and Hell or extraterrestrials, I'm warning you, I'm moving out of this shelter.
- Don't worry, Bruno objected, amused by his reaction, I'm not going to change into a pixie or some kind of evil spirit.
- So, what do you mean by "this dimension"?
- I just want to say here, now, in the life you have, that's all.
- I prefer that, because between you and me, all this is just fanciful talk.
- What then?
- All these affairs of universal energy, of the parallel world, of life after death, of multiple lives and all these idiotic ideas...
- And what do you believe in then? asked Bruno who had stopped to be more attentive to Jack's reflection.
- I don't believe in anything, that's all. We are born, we die and in between, we do what we can.
- That doesn't give much meaning to life.
- You said it yourself and, here, I agree with you: life has no meaning. I have worked throughout my existence to get what I wanted, to make my family happy, and when I finally got the results I wanted... poof, everything fell apart, and I was the first to crumble... Jack said, turning around.

Bruno looked at him, giving him time without interrupting him, waiting for the rest.

- Look, said Jack finally, after a long silence. It's pathetic, don't you think?

- No, replied Bruno, in a calm voice. But I think, even though I don't know the details of your life, you're carrying a lot of weight on your shoulders.

- What do you mean by that?

- Whether in everything you are going through now or in what you have been through in the past, I sincerely believe that you have always done your best.

- What do you mean?

- It's simple, in the misfortunes that happened to you, did you do your best *not to* succeed?

- Of course not...

- Did you do it on purpose so that everything collapses in your life, as you say?

- What a question! No, obviously not!

- So, you see, you could start with that.

- By what?

- By accepting that even if everything that you did seems to have resulted in everything falling apart, you always tried to do your best, even if you don't think you were at your best... in a way, you were.

Jack was watching Bruno, trying to discern what he meant.

- I do not understand what you're trying to say, he admitted after a moment.

- Look... life is the reflection or, if you prefer, the answer to what we are, or in other words: to what we feel.

- One moment, interrupted Jack, what exactly are you implying?

- You said that before, you had achieved everything you wanted, right?

- Yes, but I don't see the connection.

- Tell me, how did you feel at the time?

- I felt good...

- Tell me more... Explain to me how you felt inside, how you saw things, how you interpreted what you lived, the events, and everything else.

Jack's gaze revealed his suspicion. Bruno noticed it and said to him:

- Trust me, you'll judge later, okay?
- Okay, but I find you more and more strange.
- As long as I don't scare you too much, replied Bruno with an amused smile.
- It's been okay so far, replied Jack, returning the smile. So here it is: there was nothing impossible for me. If I wanted something, I would do whatever it took to get it. I was not afraid of anything, in fact, I was convinced that nothing bad could happen to me, and that if that happened, that I would find a solution to get out of it. I do not remember ever having felt any fear.
- So, in summary, everything you wanted, you felt the desire and then nothing could prevent you from achieving what you had decided, right?
- It seems like that, yes.
- So, to be sure that I understood everything, you first felt what you wanted to succeed?
- Uh... yes, that's it. I thought about it and when I really wanted to inside, I came up with lots of ideas. I then took action and put everything in place to make it work. I even remember that, from time to time, when things slowed down, I would lay on the couch in my living room and I would imagine what I wanted. A few days later, everything I had hoped for came true.

Bruno listened attentively to his comrade.

- Do you have any other questions? inquired Jack.
- Not really, said Bruno, still with that little smile. Yes, actually, he said, I do have another question.
- Go ahead, we're already this far...
- Can't you see a parallel between then and now?
- A parallel? No...
- When things started to go wrong in your life, did you act the same way?
- What do you mean?

- You said that when you imagined what you wanted, you felt it?

- Of course, otherwise I could not desire it.

- Every time?

- Yes, it was inevitable.

- What if you wanted something and you didn't feel it when you thought about it?

- Nothing happened, why?

- There it is, the parallel!

- Explain yourself...

- If I understood correctly, and I'm repeating myself, when you succeeded, everything you imagined by feeling it, happened.

- Exactly.

- Here's the parallel: when everything started to go wrong in your life, did you act the same way?

- That is to say?

- If you started to imagine the worst while being afraid of it happening, whatever it might be, what you would start to feel was fear.

- OK...

- Then, if you started to imagine the worst scenarios and think only about it by imagining what could go wrong...

- Go on...

- Like what you could imagine by feeling it, was always happening...

- You mean that...

- Does it look like what happened?

Jack looked at Bruno for a moment, got up to take the time to think, then turned to answer him:

- It looks like it, yes, and even... a lot!

The Introduction

- Wake up, we have an appointment.

Bruno, who had been standing since sunrise, tapped Jack with his foot to wake him up.

- But what could be so urgent? he asked in a sleepy voice.
- Come on, I'll explain on the way, said Bruno, picking up his bag.

Jack gathered his things in turn, then quickly joined Bruno who was already making his way down the road at high speed.

- Can you explain?
- It's our good deed day today, but before we start, we need to do this, said Bruno, showing him a poster while continuing his brisk walk.
- YMCA?
- Yes... A good clean-up would not go amiss. They have lots of very nice showers, and it's free. I am sure you will appreciate it.
- Who are you saying that to? said Jack, taking the lead to enter the building.
- We meet here, he said when they had passed the entrance to go, each in their turn, towards the showers.

Once back at the entrance of the building, both clean and dressed, Jack barely recognized Bruno. Washed hair carefully gelled to his head, beard of several days now well-trimmed; even his clothes were different.

- Where did you find these clothes? he asked.

- In my magic bag, Bruno replied, laughing while tapping the bag he was holding. I'm almost as well dressed as you are now, he noted, alluding to the new clothes that Jack was also wearing.

- Yes, an employee gave them to me in exchange for those I had. I didn't know they were doing this here.

- There are a lot of things you don't know, replied Bruno, pushing the door to go out and walk to their new destination. But tell me, how long have you been roaming the streets? You still haven't told me.

- Not very long... about two weeks, maybe more.

- And what brought you here?

- I... began Jack...

- Continue, Bruno encouraged him, I... what?

- In truth, I ran away.

- Ran away? From what? asked Bruno, stopping mid-step.

- Everything!

Bruno continued to stare at Jack, waiting for the rest.

- I suppose you would like to have more details?

- If it's not too much to ask.

- Okay, said Jack, taking a few steps to sit on a bench nearby.

Bruno followed him and took his place beside him, ready to hear the story.

<u>**The Visit**</u>

- Shame!

Jack was walking next to Bruno, who was heading for their destination, after he had told his story.

- And you have stayed out on the streets since that time? asked Bruno.
- Yes, but that was not my goal at the start. In reality, I did not know where to go. All I wanted was to find peace, to have some time and space, alone with myself.
- You certainly don't want for space here, said Bruno, pointing to the area in front of them.
- Indeed, and since the good weather and the heatwave were still going on, it was relatively easy to find a place to sleep. Then the days passed, without my noticing, until we met.
- Haven't you thought about going home?
- Yes, a few times... I don't know if you can understand, but with what was happening, I could no longer look at my family without feeling this feeling of shame; it had become unbearable... and despite the time that has passed, Jack finished studying Bruno, I feel it even more now.
- You're a little harsh on yourself, don't you think?
- Maybe, but it's stronger than me, that's how I feel. I could no longer cope with everything that was happening to me, so the only escape I found was to run away. That or end my life.

- You made the right choice then.

- There are times when I'm not so sure... But tell me: where are we going?

- Right there, replied Bruno, pointing to the illuminated sign announcing:

HOSPITAL

- What are we doing here? Asked Jack, stopping.

- Don't worry, I'm here to see a friend.

-...?

- This is the reason for our cleaning and our change of clothes. They don't let me in otherwise.

- Who is it?

- You'll see, said Bruno, going towards the building.

- He must be important to you, to do all this.

- Everyone is important, retorted Bruno, jogging across the street and leaving him behind.

After passing the reception hall, Bruno took the elevator and went directly to his friend's room. Jack was behind him and, entering in his turn, he discovered a man lying on a bed, an IV in his arm, an oxygen mask on his nose. Through the transparent plastic, he saw that the man was wearing... lipstick.

- Hello, my dear, said the man lying on the bed, displaying a broad smile despite the fatigue that permeated his voice.

- Hello, beautiful, replied Bruno, returning his smile. He took his hand and while pointing to the lipstick, he added: you seem to be in great shape today.

- Super fit, retorted the man, removing his mask. As you can see, I'm having a little fun this morning.

- Good job, said Bruno. Roby, this is Jack, the guy I already told you about.

- Pleased to meet you, said Roby, waving at him, sorry not to get up, but I feel a little lazy today.

- Roby is terminally ill, Bruno said to Jack. He has only two or three days left to live, according to medical forecasts.

- And then *bye-bye*, said Roby, coughing, I'm starting to be impatient.

Jack looked at the jovial man, stretched out on his bed, not knowing how to react, a slight discomfort beginning come over him.

- Are you okay? asked Bruno to get Jack's attention.
- Yes, yes... a little uncomfortable, I admit, but it's okay.
- I understand, said Roby, but you don't have to be, as strange as it may seem.
- Thank you, said Jack, I guess I just find it astonishing that you seem to take so the fact that you are going to die soon... if that's what I understood...
- Indeed, it may seem surprising as you say, but as I have spent too long a part of my life pretending, I am now able to see my life as it is and to accept it with all its highs and lows.
- Our friend may need some clarification, Bruno interfered, if you could help him a little to understand, it would be nice.
- Yes... of course. What do you think, Jack, would you like me to explain to you the reason why Bruno brought you here?
- Yes... that would be fine, said Jack, in an uncertain voice, looking at Bruno, who in turn glanced at Roby, who started to speak.

- So here it is: as I'm sure you've guessed, I'm gay. All my life, I repressed what I was inside of me. I have always felt an attraction towards people of the same sex as me, but coming from a good family and from a social background rather... *proud,* let's say it like that, where judgment and, above all, condemnation reigned, there was no question of admitting this... *fetish,* as some said, that I lived in secret.
- What is the link with today?
I know now that's what made me sick, said Roby.
- Being gay?
- No, not that, my cancer has nothing to do with my sexuality. It is rather the fact of having hidden it all my life.
- I'm not sure I understand...

- It is not very long since I have been able to accept who I am. In fact, I have only accepted it since the onset of my illness. I didn't want to spend the little time I have left...

Jack waited for the rest, observing Roby who was holding back his words, before continuing:

- ... Being ashamed, of who I really am!

<u>**The Feeling**</u>

Bruno looked out the window, all the while listening attentively to the conversation between Roby and Jack.

- You mean it was that feeling that made you sick?
- Maybe. No matter what feelings you carry within you, they end up, over time, having an impact on your life but also on your physical health. Whether it is cancer, a chronic disease that manifests itself, or even depression, the feelings that live in us affect our bodies. Whether negative or positive for that matter.

Roby lingered a few seconds on Jack before continuing:

- In my case, the shame and the fear of being discovered, the worry of hurting others like my family, for example, of carrying inside me the humiliation they would have experienced if my secret had been discovered, all that made me suffer inside. And when I look at what I am suffering now, I find a lot of similarities.
- Can our thoughts be so powerful?
- Much more than you can imagine. If you look at your life now, right now, and you are honest, you will find that the situation you find yourself in, (and it could be anything, because I don't know your life,) is actually the result of thoughts you've had and nurtured in the past. Whatever you wanted, or what you were afraid of... voila! You're in the middle of it now, whether you like it or not... just like me.
- But how can you be sure?
- When we approach the end, there is a kind of understanding that appears in our mind. And since I have had a lot of time to think since the beginning of my own end, I have come to understand a lot of things.

Roby paused for a moment to partially put on his oxygen mask, take a deep breath, then he returned to Jack to add:

- But the most precious lesson I learned is that no one has to lose everything to understand and change what they need to be happy.

Jack glanced at Bruno, who was silent, then focused again at Roby, feeling deeply affected by his speech, and above all astonished by the subject: the same one he had discussed with Bruno during their conversation shortly before, it was as if it was meant to be...

- And if you could change something now, he asked in an emotional voice, what would it be?
- It's a little late now, said Roby with a sad smile, but what I had to change, I did.
- Can I ask you what it was?
- Love myself, he replied, just that. Love what I am, as I am. Appreciate the beautiful things, and the not so beautiful things that I have done in my life also. To love when I have not succeeded, because in these moments, I really believed in what I was doing and, therefore, I believed in myself.

Roby took the time to wipe off the liquid dripping from his oxygen mask, then continued:

- You see, friend, what I did not understand at that time, is that we must always be proud of what we are, regardless of what we have done and the results obtained. The results against which we judge ourselves are only a measure compared to the others. It is only us who can really know if we have done everything we could, and if the answer is yes, then we must never let what we believe to be true depend be affected by anyone else's opinions.

Jack remained thoughtful, while Roby, out of breath, inhaled big puffs of air in his mask.

- Excuse me, it happens to me when I talk too much, said Roby before pausing again to take in air in his mask.
- I think we're going to let you rest, Bruno intervened, approaching the bed.

Roby thanked him with a nod, oxygen mask still over his face.

- Thank you, said Jack, taking his free hand, I appreciate it very much.
- I'll come back to see you, Bruno promised, heading for the door.
- Or maybe not... answered Roby, displaying a broad smile under his mask.

Jack turned to his friend, as if to look at him one last time.

- Or maybe not... he said, winking at him just before going out.

<u>Yo-yo</u>

-Yo... Dude!

Still troubled by his meeting with Roby, Jack was waiting, with Bruno by his side, for the traffic light to turn green so that they could cross the road and return to their shelter, when he saw the person who had called out start to walk towards them while gesturing. Nearly six feet tall, hair gathered in a bun atop his head, and a beard over a foot long, this young man, who must have been in his early thirties, had rather the appearance... of a Viking warrior.

- How are you? he went on, clapping Bruno's hands and then hugging him and lifting him off the ground.
- It will be better my feet touch solid ground again, joked Bruno stifling in the arms of the newcomer.
- I'm so glad to see you, said the stranger, after putting him down.
- Me too, said Bruno laughing, where did you go? I haven't been able to see you...
- I know, I ghosted you for a while, but I was abroad on a humanitarian mission. You know how it is, you know when you leave, but...
- Not when you come back, Bruno finished smiling, I know. Where are you located?
- Not far from here, two streets away, near the hangars and you?
- Near the bridge over there, do you want to eat with us tonight? I'll go get something good, you'll see.
- Okay, I know you know some good places, replied the young man, giving him a wink.

Jack watched the two men without saying a word. What struck him was that, despite an age difference that seemed quite significant between the two, they seemed to share the same bond.

- Let me introduce you to Jack, said Bruno, turning around and forcing Jack out of his thoughts. Jack this is Yoyo, but everyone calls him Yo.
- It's a pleasure. said Yo, shaking Jack's hand. I'm glad to meet you.
- Jack is a new friend, he has just arrived in the area.
- And you intend to stay with us for a long time? asked Yo, all smiles.

Jack looked at the young man, not knowing what to answer, and above all... not really understanding what Yoyo meant.

<u>Wealth</u>

- And like I've said before, this here is the good life, said Yo, finishing his story.

Jack had been listening to the young man tell Bruno about his humanitarian adventures for almost an hour.

- I don't bother you too much? asked Yo of Jack.
- No, actually, I think what you're talking about is very interesting. I have never had the opportunity to speak with people who have participated in humanitarian missions. Everything you've shared is very enlightening.
- Thanks.
- But if you'll permit me, what did you retain the most from all these trips or all these experiences of helping others?
- Hmm... that real wealth is not where you think it is.

The young man said these words with a particular depth in his voice, it was the first time since his arrival that he spoke with such emotion.

- Real wealth, he continued, is not visible, the real wealth of man is... inside him, not outside. And when I say man, I'm not talking about gender, but human beings.
- I suspected as much, assured Jack. But what exactly do you mean by wealth?
- What do you think?
- I'm not sure anymore... a few days ago my opinions on this subject started to change.
- Tell me if I'm wrong, but I have the impression that you are reviewing your whole understanding of values?

- You are not mistaken.

- Then... if you want, I'll tell you how I went through the same thing, and you will understand at the same time what I mean by wealth.

- Deal, said Jack, eager to hear the rest.

After glancing at Bruno, who winked at him with approval, Yo began:

- So then...

The Idea

- I'm bored, damn it!
- Go to the beach, you like water.
- No, there are too many people.
- Go to the chalet in the mountains.
- It's lame.
- Go skiing in the Alps.
- Too cold.
- It's crazy, don't you think, Yo? Your father is stuffed with money, you get a bigger pension than most people who work full time, you can do whatever you want, *literally no limit*, and there is nothing that interests you.
-Oh yeah? Let's talk about that, it's been at least two years since I last saw him, some father...
- Are you going to keep hanging on to this for a long time?
- Whatever...
- Here, said his friend, handing him a copy of the newspaper he had read while waiting for him on the terrace of the cafe where they were seated. All you have left is to go to Hell!

Yo took the newspaper whose headline read in bold letters:

EVERYTHING TO BE REBUILT, CONDITIONS WORSE THAN HELL

- What happened? he asked, browsing the article that spoke about a natural disaster in a developing country on the African continent.
- It would give you a change you from all that luxury, anyway.

Yo was still reading the article when suddenly it clicked in his mind.

- You're... right...he finally said, cutting out the article to put it in his pocket. I know someone who works for a humanitarian organization and she has been asking me for months to participate in a mission.
- And. .?
- I'll call her.
- Why?
- To get more information.
- Do you want to go to a poor country?
- Yes, replied Yo, returning the rest of the newspaper to him. I have something I need to do... to settle.
- Hey, calm down, said his friend, it was a joke.
- Ha ha ha, Yo feigned laugher, picking up his things. I'm still laughing!
- Are you serious? insisted his friend, surprised by his reaction.
- Very... She's talked to me about it several times, I think the time has come. With that, I bid you goodbye, and if we don't see each other soon, it will be because I will be...in hell, as it says in the newspaper.
- As you wish, replied his friend still in shock, then raising his glass added: I wish you much happiness and may God be with you!

Yo got up and paid the waiter for their drinks, then he turned to his friend smiling and said:

- Or maybe the devil...!

The Offer

- I'm out of here!

Though he had arrived in Central Africa only a few days ago, Yo was ready to leave. He picked up his bag and went to sit at the transport departure stand.

- Where are you going like that? asked the boss, responsible for the area, who had followed him.
- Home, replied Yo, turning around.
- Why?
- Because it's not at all what I expected to find when I came here.
- And what did you expect to find?
- A difference...
- And?
- And... nothing. That's it, I'm going home!
- And when do you plan to get there?
- Why do you ask?
- Because the next transport is in a week... and you don't have a lot of water, well, surely not enough to last a week, said the man, indicating a single bottle atop his luggage.

Yo looked at him without answering.

- Look, said the boss... maybe you didn't understand what it is that we're doing here. Come back and I'll show you... Give me a week, just one, and then if you still want it, I'll tell you how to get home without delay.

The man looked at him with an expression that seemed sincere. Yo glanced over at the arid desert that lay before him and figured he didn't have enough water to last that long.

- Okay, he agreed finally, but afterwards, you have to tell me how to get back, promise?
- Promise, said the boss, turning around to head back, a smile on the corner of his lips.

<u>**Surveillance**</u>

- You'll start with this!

The boss had just finished giving the morning class given to the young children of the village. And now they had only one thing on their minds: play time.

- Just that? asked Yo to be sure.
- Yes, your responsibility is to watch them play.
- Why? They don't need me to play.
- They don't need you to play, they need you to protect them.
- What? No there's risk of them being run over, the only car I've seen in days is falling apart, buried in the sand over there.
- That's not it, replied the boss, smiling at his reply. Sometimes there are big bush cats that come out in search of food, and a pack of children with no cares in the world, just having fun, is an easy target.
- And what do I do if I see one? cried Yo to the boss, but he was already gone, too far to answer him.

The rest of the day passed quickly for the children, but slowly for Yo, who kept scanning the surroundings for any potential source of danger.

The Request

- So how did you like your experience? asked the boss after having sent the children back to their parents at the end of the day.
- No problem, everything went well.
- Very well, he said, tapping him on the shoulder, you will do that again tomorrow.
- Yo's pain and objections were lost on the boss who had turned and was already walking away.

The following days, apart from a few small manual jobs, most of his time was spent watching over the children and the outside world around them. On two occasions, he even happened to spot suspicious movements in the undergrowth, which he went to check, taking care to make much noise to scare off a potential four-footed attacker, but found nothing. He about to start the beginning of a new day when...

- You are doing well!
- Thank you, Yo replied to his boss who joined him. At this rate, I will soon be able to draw up a complete plan of the landscape... nonexistent.

The boss laughed, then said to him:

- You know what? I like your sense of humor. I feel like I'm seeing you in a whole new light. I never suspected that...
- That's nice of you, but I would like to know something.
- What is it?
- Did you ask me to stay here just to play babysitter?

- Well, actually, I came to ask you to do something else today. You see the group of women over there who do the refueling? They asked me if you could accompany them today.

- Me, why?

- Usually they have their own guide, but this morning he is unwell, and since they think you are a good guardian, they asked me if you were available.

- And what am I supposed to do?

- Watch for a possible danger, as you do here.

Yo took the time to examine the group of women who were happily talking to each other, laughing out loud.

- Why not, he said finally, it seems like fun and it will give me a change. When do we leave?

- They're already ready, they're just waiting for you.

- Let's go, then, said Yo, heading towards the group.

The boss watched him go... with a smile.

The Walk

- Are we almost there yet?

The group had been walking for two hours and Yo began to feel his fatigue start to take over, especially since he had no idea where their destination was. They had only explained to him that his role was to watch the surroundings, just in case...

- No, no, replied, the youngest of the women with her particular accent, who seemed to be the leader.
- No, no, what? asked Yo.
- No, no, we're not coming soon, replied the woman, laughing, immediately followed by the others.
- Can we at least stop a bit then?
- Yes, yes, she replied, laughing again, while continuing to walk briskly, followed by the laughter of the other women.

Damn it! Yo thought to himself while continuing to follow, but what do they have to laugh about so much? Since we left, all they do is talk a little, and then burst into laughter when they look at me. Then they start singing! They talk again a little more, what's worse it's in a language that I don't even know, look at me, nearly choke of laughter and sing again. I've had it up to here...

- What's your name? asked the girl who seemed to lead the group, interrupting his brooding.
- Yoyo, he replied.

He had barely pronounced his name when the girl repeated it to the others, so much so that it was soon on the lips of all the women who laughed while singing... *Yoyoun, Yoyoun*, laughing *louder*.

- Here, she said turning to him, Yoyoun, you have an African name now. Mine is Odede, by the way. I will introduce my companions to you later, but I warn you, they do not speak your language.

- But you do...

- I learned in a school that no longer exists now. But I continued learning with the people who have come to help us.

- So, if I understand correctly, you are the leader of the group?

- No, not exactly, she said, translating his supposition to her colleagues who burst out laughing. There is no leader here, everyone is on equal footing.

- Oh well, I thought... because of...

- I am the only one who can exchange with you, the others will not speak to you directly, that is perhaps what gives this impression.

- I understand better now. Can you tell me how long it takes to walk before arriving?

- About... two hours, more or less.

- Two plus two equals four. Four hours of walking just to get there! Are we going to sleep there?

Before answering, she took the time to translate to her companions. Her words elicited a general burst of laughter from the group, which did not come as a great surprise to... Yoyoun.

- No, we don't sleep there, replied Odede, holding back her laughter, but it'll be a little slower when we get back. After all these hours of walking in the sun, the girls tend to be slower, she said, immediately translating to her companions, who laughed.

- And can I know where we're going? Yo asked, taking a sip of water from his almost empty gourd, pouring the rest out on the ground, finding it too hot.

Odede looked at him for a moment before continuing, with a courteous smile:

- To get what you just poured out!

The Stop

- It's time to rest.

Yo did not answer immediately; he was busy observing the various travelers who had arrived at the water supply point. Mostly women, accompanied by a few men, from different tribes.

- Do they come from far away? he asked Odede, who was seated next to him, enjoying a little patch of shade.
- About as far as we have come.
- But is there no water closer to the villages?
- Yes, but it was contaminated a long time ago. The only drinking water left is here. Do you see these men with guns? she said, pointing to them. They are the guards.
- Of the water point?
- Right. Day and night, they take turns. Each village participates.
- What would happen if this water point disappeared?
- Imminent death. These guards you see there, are ready to give their lives to protect this place.
- That much?
- They made a promise. They know that if this water point disappears, their families, their parents, their children, their friends, all those they love will disappear, and they have understood for a long time that without them, their life would be in vain. That everything would have to be started again, every time, indefinitely. This is what gives meaning to their lives, what they do and why they do it. It is important in our culture, to give a meaning to our life, is it not the same for you?

Yo contemplated without answering all these people who helped each other and busied themselves collecting water in leather pockets, then leaving for their long walks back... singing.

- And why do you always sing? You sing while walking, working, and for no reason at all... You should form a choir while you are at it.
- It's to come together... said Odede with a laugh. You're funny, you know that?
- Uh... I'll take your word for it, said Yo, a little taken aback, but delighted with the comment.
- You see, singing is a way to unite. When we unite our voices, the vibration it creates gives us new energy, like a kind of communion, it breaks loneliness. You know what it is... loneliness?
- I thought so, but I have begun to discover a side that I did not know about before.
- Ah, yes?
- Yes, the loneliness that you create for yourself...

Yo continued to admire these people who supported each other while simply going about their business, appreciating the beauty that emanated from each of their gestures, as small as they were; he could see and feel such gratitude from these people for each thing that they received or that they were giving to others. And despite all the difficulties he saw in the lives of these people, they seemed to remember only the good.

- I'm sorry, he went on, for what I did earlier, when I emptied my gourd...
- It's ok, you didn't know. Water is very precious here, for us it is worth much more than gold.
- I know it now. And how long do you have with what you bring back?
- One day.
- Just that?

- Yes, what we bring back is for the whole village. Tomorrow will be the same, and the day after that... Each day, in turn, a group comes here, it is essential to our survival. Is there nothing like that where you come from?

- Like what? asked Yo, lost in his observations.

- Something so important that you dedicate your life to it?

- Yeah, Yo answered vaguely, thinking about all the money he had wasted, but it is certainly not as precious as everything I have discovered these days.

- Ah, and what is so precious, where you live?

- Something...

Odede looked at him, waited a moment and understood, seeing his sad look, that their discussion had ended.

The Race

- So Yoyoun, ready for another mission this morning?

Yo, or Yoyoun, turn to look at his boss, all smiles.

- I see that news travels fast here.
- Especially the funny ones. With a name like that, I'm sure nothing can stop you.
- I'm invincible now.
- So how was your experience?
- Another world is opening up to me, especially thanks to the discussions I had with Odede.
- An extraordinary woman... She told you that she had refused an important position within an organization?
- No, what kind of position?
- An international representative position.
- She preferred to stay here in this little village in the middle of nowhere? Why?
- For love, my friend.
- She has a spouse, then?
- No... she lives alone, if you can call it alone, because she is very well surrounded.
- By love for whom then?
- Out of love for... herself.

Yo looked at his boss, hoping for more explanation.

- You can talk to her about it when you return if you want, he continued changing the subject, but for the moment you have a race to run, that's what I came to talk to you about.
- All right, what is it?

- There is a man who lives alone, in the forest, about ten kilometers from here.

- Some kind of hermit?

- If you want, yes. He is a friend of the village and we bring him a few things from time to time.

- And you want me to go.

- Bullseye. I told myself that after your walk yesterday, this wouldn't even faze you, especially since it's just over there, Bruno assured him, pointing to a little drop in the distance, you just have to go straight, no chance you will get lost.

- And how do I find it? Are there tree numbers?

- Don't worry, replied the boss, amused, you will find him.

- Okay, and what should I take him?

- This... he said, presenting a small, carefully wrapped package.

Yo took the object in one hand and examined it, intrigued.

- Is that all?

- That's all he needs for the moment.

- OK, Yo replied without trying to find out more, picking up his water bottle and backpack to start walking in the direction indicated. See you soon, he called, I will deliver this for you in record time.

- If you say so... Oh, and watch out for the big cats!

- Don't worry, he said, giving him a wave, I'm Yoyoun the invincible now.

The Hermit

When he got close to the forest, Yo spied a half-naked man sitting on the stump of dead tree, observing him closely.

- You should take better care of your physical health, said the man, when the young man had gotten closer, you look like you're out of breath.
- But you're white! Yo exclaimed, ignoring the man's remark.
- Yes, so what? What did you expect to see? A Tibetan monk sitting in a snowbank?
- No, maybe more a black African, sitting on... perhaps a rock?
- Sorry to disappoint you, said the man. Do you have something for me?
- Yes, hold on, said Yo, handing him the small package.
- Thank you, replied the man, slipping the package into his pocket without saying anything else.
- ...?
- ...What? Do you want a tip? asked the false monk, looking at Yo, who was looking at him.
- Not really... and honestly now that I see you, I can tell that the tip wouldn't be that great anyway.

The man remained as still as a stone, unmoving.

- But before I go, said Yo, taking a seat near the man to rest a little, I would still like to understand what you are doing here.
- Nothing!
- Why?
- To learn.
- But what do you mean?
- What is real loneliness, being alone with yourself.

- You are in the right place, judging by the proximity of your neighbors.

- And you, little comedian, do you know what it's like to be alone with yourself?

- Strangely, I have started to discover a different side of loneliness since I have been here.

- To use your own words, "But what do you mean?"

- Since I have been here, I have been surrounded by people... who are *real*, people who ask for nothing and who offer what little they have without asking for anything or expecting anything in return.

An imperceptible smile appeared on the hermit's lips, as if he saw something being born in the young man.

- And where is the link? he asked, wishing to find out more from his visitor.

- I know much better how to be alone with others than with myself. Before I came here, I thought I didn't feel this loneliness. Well... I camouflaged it relatively well with everything I could find. I kept busy until I got dizzy. In reality, I had become a master of isolation, not wanting to look at my life as it was, not wanting to realize that the life I was leading was not at all like what I would have liked it to have been.

He paused for a moment, remembering how he had been just a few weeks earlier, before continuing:

- And it is since I am here, that I have felt the most loneliness ... that I lived there, he concluded thinking about where he had come from, his gaze lost in the horizon.

- And what do you want to do now?

- Go home before the sun goes down, he replied, rising to his feet. I have a few hours of reflection before me! So, I wish you... nothing, in fact, after all, that's what you seem to want.

- You understand me well, said the hermit, standing up in his turn to shake his hand. Tell the one who sent you that the door is wide open, he will understand. And don't forget, he added slyly: life is made of little things.

Yo set off in the direction of the village. The hermit, who was holding his package in his hand, shouted after him smiling:

- And thank you for the matches!

<u>Odede and...</u>

- Hello, how are you this morning?

Odede was standing in the doorway of the small room which served as both a meeting room and a cafeteria.

- Better and better, Yo replied, but aren't you already on your way to the water point?
- The departure was delayed, so I thought I might come to see you.
- That's nice of you, but why was the departure delayed?
- We saw a pack of wild beasts. The men left to scout the area.
- Is it serious?
- No, no, it happens often. They will push them back far enough so that we can pass safely.
- Yesterday, the boss told me that you refused a proposal to work abroad, Yo said changing the conversation, is it true?
- In reality, explained Odede taking a seat in front of him, I accepted the offer, then I resigned.
- Oh well, I understood something else.
- I thought that with that assignment, I would be able to better help my people. I thought that I would find in the outside world what was missing here.
- And it was not the case?
- No. I rather discovered that it was the opposite: it is what is here that is missing to the outside world.

Yo considered this serene, playful woman, who seemed happy despite the poverty that reigned there.

- And what is it exactly that is missing?

- What you've started to appreciate since you've been here, she replied with a smile. Haven't you discovered new things since your arrival?

- Lots, and more every day. So much so that now I'm looking forward to the morning to see what the boss has in store for me.

Odede smiled, then she slipped a hand into her pocket to take out an envelope.

- You see, it's easy... I hope we will have other opportunities to discover many things together, she said standing up, handing him the envelope. Here, the boss asked me to give you that, she said before leaving.

Surprised, Yo took the envelope and opened it to find... a round-trip ticket. After a few minutes of staring at the ticket in his hands, he went out, and slowly crossed the small village to meet the boss who was busy watching for the arrival of a transport truck.

- How are you this morning? he yelled over the noise of the trucks.
- I have a message for you from the hermit: he wants you to know that 'the door is wide open.' According to him, you will understand.

A smile of restrained satisfaction appeared on the man's face

- I'm delighted, he said, lowering his voice now that the truck had stopped.
- Is it transport for the return? asked Yo, glancing at the heavyweight.
- Exactly. Are you ready to go home? As soon as the truck is ready, you will just have to get on board and the driver will take you to the station.
- Is that all? said Yo. I jump on board and it's over...
- It looks like it... Yes. Isn't that what you wanted?

- I thought so... conceded Yo, stroking his ticket, but in reality... no, he finished. I don't know exactly what I want anymore, but I know one thing, he said raising up his head to look the boss in the eyes. Well... whatever it is that I want, I haven't quite found it yet.

The two men looked at each other, Yo turning the envelope he was holding in his hands.

- And if you're alright with it... I would prefer not to use this, he blurted out, handing him the ticket.
- Are you sure?
- Certain! Yo confirmed, letting go of his return ticket.
- I warn you, the next departure is in over a month.
- I am no longer in a hurry, assured the young man by looking at the landscape around him. I still have so much to discover and understand that I am convinced that I will not see time pass.
- Alright then, it's a deal, said the boss, holding out his hand.
Deal, Yo confirmed, squeezing it. But since we're going to be together for a while, he said slightly hesitantly, I'd love to know what I can call you, if it's not a... secret.

The boss laughed, then replied:

- Do what you like. But if you want... you can call me Bruno!

__The Return__

- And I stayed there for four months... the first time.

Yo finished recounting his first experience of his humanitarian missions.

- And have you gone back since? asked Jack.
- A few times, yes.
- There is something I don't understand: if your parents are so rich, what are you doing on the street?

Yo glanced at Bruno before continuing:

- When I returned, many things had changed in my mind and in the way that I saw life. I just couldn't wait to show my friends the man I had become. But... it didn't go over as I had imagined.
- What happened?
- I went directly to the house of my best friend at the time, but that day he was holding a get together with all of his other friends. When he saw me in the dilapidated clothes of a humanitarian volunteer with long braided hair and a long, badly trimmed beard, he intercepted me before anyone else saw me and pulled me aside. He said he was glad I was back, but that it wasn't a good time for me to be there. He said he would be delighted to meet in the evening, once the party was over.
- What did you do?

- I left, a little in shock. I did not really understand what was going on. Everything was so different. I no longer recognized the world I had left just a few months ago. I sat on a park bench to think; I watched people who passed without seeing me, all in a hurry to find and obtain wealth. In short, I was able to see the side of life that I had left behind. And yet on the other hand, I saw in this same park, people living in the street, without money or possessions, who were speaking to each other, supporting and helping each other.

- What did you do next?

- I stayed on the bench until night, watching life take its course in front of me, not really knowing what to do. The world I had left and the one I had found were so different... Then, I couldn't tell you what time it was, a homeless man came to see me to ask me if I needed something, he told me that if I was in a really tight spot, he could help me.

- Like you did with me, Jack commented, looking at Bruno. He turned back to Yo, "and then?"

- Then? I'm still here, trying to help those who want help, when I'm not on my humanitarian trips. This is my life, the path I have chosen. It is one of the things I have learned: we always live according to the choices we make... Like you do...

Jack turned his gaze to the distance. The words 'like you do' echoed in his head, and he realized that, subconsciously, this had always been the case, even at that very moment. What he was going through, he had decided on his own. He glanced at Bruno before continuing.

- I still find it strange to reject all this money that you could use here.

- As I told you, said Yo standing up to leave, often the real wealth is not where it seems to be, but rather in what we believe is valuable. The people you have known since your arrival do not need money as much as being recognized, helped and above all loved. You know, money is not that difficult to find. What is rare, however, is to find human beings with time and love to offer...

- Like you and Bruno?

- I'd say so... and here, that's what is worth more than gold.

With that, Yo hugged Bruno, and shook hands firmly with Jack, who stepped back on the piece of cardboard that served as his bed to let him pass.

The Difference

- Why are you here?

Bruno turned to see Jack watching him, obviously waiting for an answer.

- Can you be a little more precise?
- I thought I could find answers by staying here, but I end up with even more questions.
- Sorry, I know I'm repeating myself, but can you be more precise?

Jack looked at him with a bewildered look.

- It is important that your questions be precise, Bruno continued.
- OK... let me try again. If I understood Yo's story correctly, the Bruno he talked about and you are the same...
- So?
- Yes or no?
- Well... Yes!
- And like him, your life on the street, is voluntary?
- One could say that.
- Yes or no?
- Yes.
- Why?

Bruno looked at Jack, without answering...

- I find it hard to understand because I see all these people who are struggling to survive, who sleep outside because they have nothing left, and somehow you find it... almost pleasant to live like this... Why?

- I'll help you understand, but first, let me show something, Bruno said calmly.

He got up and motioned for Jack to follow him to other side of the bridge under which they had been camped for a few days. After a few minutes of silent walking, he sat himself on a large flat stone at the edge of the river.

- Sit down, he said, pointing to a space near him.

- What is it today? Jack retorted, taking his place. A zen meditation class to the sound of flowing water?

- You are truly irreplaceable, said Bruno smiling. I will miss you when you are gone.

Jack looked at him with questioning eyes, surprised at his reply.

- Do you really think that you will spend the rest of your life wandering the streets? continued Bruno, staring at him. Everything you are experiencing right now is only temporary.

- Ah yes... and you predict that I'll be here for how long, Mister Expert?

- Until you know why, replied Bruno, staring at him.

- Know why, what?

- Why you are here... Look, said Bruno after a silence, turning to the river. Do you see these birds?

- Of course...

- How are they different from us?

- Sorry?

- What do they have that *you* don't have?

Jack looked at the birds, trying to understand.

- Feathers?

- That's a start, smiled Bruno, keep going.

- I don't see the point...
- Okay... What do *you* have, that they don't have?

Jack focused again on the birds, trying to discover the undiscoverable.

- Have you ever seen one starving to death because he had nothing to eat? Bruno asked him.
- Uh... I must admit that I have not.
- Have you ever seen one who seemed worried?
- Not really, no.
- Have you ever seen one who was concerned with where he would find shelter or how he would feed his young, or anything else ultimately?
- ... I don't think so, no, replied Jack, turning his gaze to Bruno.
- Look at the one who has only one leg, do you have the impression that he is more unhappy than the others, same for the one who is missing a wing tip, does he seem desperate to you?
- No, actually.
- I spent a lot of time sitting here watching these birds, trying to understand, trying to find out what they had that I didn't have.

Jack listened, not daring to interrupt him.

- I too, continued Bruno, like you, I too faltered because I couldn't manage to do one thing: <u>Accept</u>. But, he said pointing to the birds, they do it naturally.
- Have you lost everything?
- In a way, yes. As you can see, you are not the first one here, he said pointing to the other makeshift shelters scattered far away, all their stories are alike, like yours, like mine.
- ...?
- What makes the difference, said Bruno, observing the silence of his friend, between those who stay and those who get back up and get out, is very simple... it's called *acceptance*.

Bruno looked at Jack who did not say a word, before continuing:

- And as long as you cannot accept your life as it is, not as you think it should be or as you would like it to be; but *as it is,* you will not be able to change anything, and more and more your life will continue in the direction that it's currently heading.

Jack contemplated the water of the river, while an interior battle raged inside him.

- Truthfully, insisted Bruno, the most difficult for you now is to be able to accept yourself as you are now. Unable to do more, unable to find all the solutions, no longer indestructible, in short... vulnerable. The most important and difficult fight you have to win is not to find solutions to the problems you have, but to admit that you can't accept that you are no longer capable of doing everything by yourself and that you need help.

Jack jumped up and left in a fury, walking in the opposite direction from which they had come.

Acceptance

- Is someone sleeping late this morning?

Bruno recognized his friend's voice and came out of his shelter.

- I sleep much better since there is no one snoring by my side, he replied with a smile, holding out his hand. Did you have good a vacation?
- Yes, it's always good to get away for a while. Especially when the weather is nice, said Jack, smiling too.
- Where did you go?
- Not very far, to tell the truth, just to the end of the bridge. With last week's temperatures, we slept better outside.
- Indeed, Bruno confirmed. Sorry for our last conversation, but...
- It's okay, Jack cut him off, I needed to hear it. Even if I didn't want to... that's what I needed.
- OK... And how do you feel now?
- Good. I have started to make peace with my life, and I sent some news to my family.

Bruno, who had sat on a block of cement nearby, looked at him without adding anything, waiting to hear what he would say next.

- The day before I left home, Jack explained, taking a seat near him, I had a discussion with my wife. I explained to her that I needed to be alone to try to understand what was going wrong in my life, that I would be away for some time, that I would send her news and that she shouldn't worry. The morning of my departure, I left her a note asking her not to look for me. I said that I would contact her myself.

- I understand.

- When I left you the other day it wasn't until the next morning that calm returned to my mind and I started to realize all kinds of things- including the fact that I had not given my wife any news for a long time. So, I left a message on her voicemail to let her know that I was still alive and in good hands.

- That was a good thing to do. But why did you come back? You could have gone home.

- Because I found your summer chalet very comfortable, joked Jack, pointing to the shelter, but above all because... Even if I found a little calm, I still have not completely accepted what is happening to me and... I need help... he admitted in a trembling voice, before turning to Bruno to add: and I think you are the best person to help me with that... well if you don't mind.

Bruno glanced at the river which was flowing calmly, then turned to Jack, looking at him straight in the eyes.

- Very well, but it will not be easy... nor really difficult either. What do you want to start with?

- I admit that since my meeting with Yo, I still do not understand very well what you do in the street, why you were in Africa and what you did there. I see you here like this, yet, life seems to be beautiful to you. I would like to know where everything you tell me comes from and which seems so simple to you.

- It's a deal. I will try to explain to you the "why" behind what I do... But first, tell me one thing: aren't you hungry?

- Yes... a little... Why?

- Because I know an excellent place which, at this precise hour, is in the very act of getting rid of delicious surpluses.

With that, Bruno got up and took a quick step, followed in spite of himself, by Jack.

Clarification

- You were right, Jack commented in reference to the dishes they had just shared, it was very good, but please, continue what you were saying.

Bruno took one last bite and put what was left in his bag. Jack, who listened to him attentively, did the same. Installed at a picnic table in a small urban park, near the restaurant where they had stocked up on food from the food scraps bin, Bruno had been doing his best to explain "his why" for a while now.

- *Everything you flee will follow you wherever you go*, is what a tribal chief once told me, because what you flee from is inside you... it's *the part of yourself that you don't know*.
- What did it mean?
- At that time, not much, but since he was a wise man, he did not add anything- allowing me to understand by myself. He knew that you don't learn with words, but with the experiences you have.
- What does that mean?
- That words constitute knowledge, and knowledge, the understanding of what you have experienced, of what you have felt.
- Okay...so?
- I told you earlier that my life turned upside down when I lost someone very dear to me, someone I loved very much, and that I had a lot of trouble to get back on my feet.
- Yes...
- I only thought about that. I was so shattered and angry that I stopped taking care of my business. I was so unable to accept the injustice of life, that I eventually fell into total depression...

- You have never mentioned your depression, but I understand, because I also feel a bit like that these day...

- I thought that by changing the scenery, the situation, what I hoped to get away from by losing myself in Africa, would allow me to escape the pain I was experiencing. But I found that it went with me wherever I went.

- What now?

- It's still like that, but different at the same time.

- How is it different?

- There is no more suffering, I learned to accept. The part that struck me the most from the chief's words, and the thing that I needed to discover was: *the part of myself that I didn't know*.

- But what exactly is this *unknown self*?

- It's the unconscious part of what you are. Life needs balance, actually, it *is* balance. There is always an opposite or a complement to everything. High-low, black-white, hot-cold, front-back, life-death, etc. In what we are, there is the conscious and the unconscious.

Jack clung to Bruno's words to be sure not to miss anything.

- To help you understand better, I must tell you first, that after my return I discovered a line of thought called 'Neuroscience.' According to Neuroscientists, most of our life is spent in our subconscious, and only a small part of our life is spent consciously. But I will not hide from you that the old tribes, without explaining it in this way, have already known all this for centuries.

- And what's the difference?

- All that we are, that is to say our personality, comes from what we have learned since birth. Your beliefs, your values, what you believe is possible or not, true or not, do not come from you, but from what others have taught you. Whether it's your parents, your teachers, your friends... What you have become is the result of what others have shown you to be.

- One moment, said Jack, you mean that I don't know what I'm doing?

- Sort of... Yes.

- OK, I admit that maybe right now, I don't really know. But I used to know, that's for sure.

- No more than now, replied Bruno, why do you think you are so lost right now?

- I await your answer, O Great Spirit...

- All our life, we react to what happens to us with the data that is stored in the unconscious part of ourselves, what we have learned from others. But when a situation arises and we cannot get the answers in this part which we call our subconscious, because there is no reference to it - for lack of experience or learning-, we start to create answers by what I call assemblages of fractions.

- Fractions? You mean I am... split?

- Yes... and no, replied Bruno, amused by the idea, listen to what I'm saying.

- That's all I ever do...

- If we have no experience corresponding to what we are looking for, continued Bruno, still amused by the commentary, our brain will manufacture responses, if you will, or create solutions by assembling parts of several similar experiences from what we have experienced. These answers or solutions may be incomplete, but still become true for us, when we constantly think about them and repeat them. We act then, on bases which are only partially true and not necessarily in agreement with what we desire.

Jack stared at the floor, trying to assemble the pieces of the puzzle that formed in his head.

- Everything we do, Bruno continued, is managed by our subconscious or, if you prefer, *the self you don't know.*

- But I feel like I'm constantly thinking, Jack protested, and I seem to be always aware of what I'm doing.

- That's exactly why, replied Bruno.

- I don't understand...

- Let me give you an example: when you walk, do you think of each step you take?

- No...

- When you are driving, do you happen to chat at the same time and realize, after several miles, that you did not consciously pay attention to your gestures?

- I imagine so.

- When you eat, do you think about your digestion? When you move, get up, sit down, pick things up, finally with each action you perform in a day, do you think before you act?

Jack shook his head.

- Whenever you occupy your conscious mind with something, like now, it is your subconscious which takes over for all that which you do not consciously think of. You could call it... your autopilot. And as you think almost all the time, as you say, it will direct your life by following the data he finds, that is to say, what you have learned during your life, whether positive or negative, it makes no difference, whether you like it or not. You already know how to do everything and your subconscious, manages it all.

- Wow...

- And the same goes for your fears, your certainties, your beliefs, your values, everything is already there, said Bruno, tapping his temple with his index finger.

Jack took a moment to reflect in silence before resuming...

- And it was your tribal chief who taught you all this?

- Yes and no, replied Bruno. Like I told you, he also knew all that, but in a different way. For my part, after my return, I went back to school and it was at that time that I made the link.

- Did you go back to university?

- Yes, some sort of catch-up. I had already done great studies before, and I kind of undertook a specialty but, this time in an area that really fascinated me: the human being. The time I spent there allowed me, with the help of those I told you about, to heal my wounds and to want to find new meaning in my life, which I am doing now.

- OK, said Jack, requesting a break by putting up his hand. I need some time to think, he explained, standing up. I'm going to walk a little if you don't mind, I don't know why, but I feel all mixed up inside, he added, gesturing with his hand from his head to his heart. I'll join you later, okay?
- No problem, we'll continue another time.

Jack walked away slowly, followed unknowingly by two squirrels.

__Reason__

- The two over there, standing apart from the rest.

Hidden behind a tree with Bruno, Jack pointed to his two children in the schoolyard in the distance.

- I come to see them regularly, he told him, it makes me feel better.

Bruno's eyes passed from children to Jack, but he made no comment. They stayed there until the children went back inside.

- Do you remember, said Jack after the children had completely disappeared from his sight, when I told you that the only choices that seemed possible to me before we met were either that I disappear or that I end my life?
- Yes, I remember it very well.
- It is because of them that I did not make the second choice. I did not want them to have abandonment and resignation as role models when they had to face the trials of life.

Bruno listened in silence; he in no way wanted to disturb Jack's reflections. He understood only too well the importance of what he was going through.

- And now, said Jack, it is for them that I continue to fight so hard for a chance to get out of this. They deserve better... he stammered, looking at Bruno with sadness.

Bruno took him in his arms and whispered in his ear:

- You too deserve better, my friend... you too!

A Strange Encounter

- It's like cats... I love cats!

Bruno and Jack were waiting in line at the soup kitchen.

- What is like cats? inquired Jack.
- It is easy to understand, in fact, replied the man in front of them, looking at them haggardly. Then he turned away and went to be served at the counter.

Jack watched him go, taken aback. Strangely clothed, not like most of the people he had known for some time, but rather as if he came from...a fairy tale. Dressed in worn 19th century style clothes, and complemented by a ponytail and a leather jacket, the man had spoken with an unusual accent which required one to pay close attention to what he said.

- Do you think it comes from his subconscious? he asked Bruno, just to tease him.
- Who knows? replied the latter, giving him a knowing wink.
- So, said Jack turning around after the eccentric man had moved away, you still haven't told me why you live on the street. Honestly, I admit that after what you told me, I understand even less.
- It's a choice, answered Bruno, it's my way of giving back, but we'll talk about it another time if you don't mind. Right now, something much more interesting is happening.

Bruno stepped forward to be served, then left to sit at the same table as the man with the ponytail.

- What did you want to say about cats? Bruno asked the man, after Jack had joined them.

He turned to answer, and it was only then that they noticed a strange gleam in his eyes.

- They have several lives, replied the man in a confident tone.
- So what? prodded Jack.
- When we say that they have several lives, they do not start a different one each time. They always continue the same existence, but as a renewal, on new grounds, with knowledge they have accumulated, but also, and above all, with the understanding of what led them to supposedly lose one. It's easy to understand, right? I love cats! he exclaimed, standing up and cutting the conversation short.

Amazed, Jack followed him until he disappeared from his sight, then asked Bruno:

- Do you know him?
- No!
- Have you seen him before?
- No!
- Where does he come from?
- No idea!
- Did you understand something?
- No, but since there are no coincidences...
- Why are you saying that?
- Because there is a reason for everything, even if we do not understand at the moment, and as what we are experiencing is a kind of affinity ...
- What? You mean we have a connection with that guy?

- What happens to us is always in harmony with what we are or at least a part. This is what is wonderful, we only have to pay attention to what is happening to us and make the link. Life always speaks to us, if we can listen and be patient.
- And where did you learn that? In your remedial college classes?

An ironic smile painted on Bruno's face when he replied:

- No... I told you: in a tribe!

The Decision

- I think I'm ready for a stay with a distant African tribe!

Bruno looked at Jack questioningly. They had been sitting on a bench for a good hour, quietly watching the people in silence, when Jack had suddenly said these words.

- Explain yourself, Bruno prodded.
- I've been listening to you trying to explain to me all these things that you learned in your African tribe, and when I think back to your friend Yoyo and his humanitarian trips, which also took place in Africa, I realize that it may be there that I will find my answers.

Bruno exploded with laughter while looking at Jack, who was surprised by his reaction.

- You don't have to travel so far to understand everything that you are trying to make sense of, Bruno assured him. Despite what you seem to believe, it is not only in my travels that I have learned what I share with you, but rather in my life in general. If I had been more open, less withdrawn in those days, I could have understood all of this right here, with the people who were already trying to help me.
- Did you get help?
- Of course, well, people tried, but I didn't want help; I was too stuck in what I believed to be my unjustifiable misfortunes. But you, Bruno continued, staring him in the eyes, you can do better!

Jack looked at him for a moment, then turned his gaze to a squirrel who was snooping around on the ground in search of a forgotten treasure. It was as if he was frozen in time, reflecting. Then, as if lost in thought, with an almost inaudible voice, he said:

- It's like that squirrel ...
- Sorry?
- I'm like that squirrel. I search everywhere hoping to find a treasure that...
- What?
- You may be right, exclaimed Jack. I believe that... I just understood something important.
- Oh really?
- Yes... I do not really know why... Perhaps thanks to everything we have exchanged since our meeting or what you just said, but there was one thing in particular that struck me recently and it just clicked in my head.
- What is it?
- The man and his thing about the cats.
- Go on, said Bruno, intrigued.
- Do you remember when he said that cats had several lives and that it was not a new life that they were starting again, but indeed the same one that continued, only better?
- Yes, so what?
- I saw myself and I suddenly understood that it was not by fleeing that my life would be better, but by continuing it... like cats, with what I had understood from the past. What I have been doing for a while is living in the past instead of living in the present doing my best to change what I can.

Bruno looked at him without saying a word, a small smile of appreciation emerging from the corner of his lips.

- You have helped me a lot to accept things, Jack continued, and I thank you. I'm not really sure how it happened, but I can feel it in here, he said, patting his chest. I also realized, after showing you my children, that my place is with those who love me... no matter how... As you said, what I try to flee goes with me wherever I go!

- Why are you telling me this?

- I think... I'm going to go home, replied Jack.

- Do you feel ready to face what awaits you?

- I'm about to find out. I will probably never be quite ready anyway. Something has changed, I'm not sure what, but I'm sure of one thing now, that my place is there with my family.

- I completely agree with you.

- You know, I also thought a lot about our visit to your friend Roby in the hospital and what he said.

- Yes. I remember.

- I understand what he meant about shame, because I felt the same thing, and even if I don't quite know what to do yet, I don't want to experience this feeling anymore. I did my best with what I had, and I don't have to be ashamed of that, that is what I understood thanks to your friend. As for the rest... I will do what I can, and we will see.

- High five! said Bruno, raising his hand.

- Can I come back to see you? asked Jack, striking his friend's palm. I have not yet really absorbed everything about why I ended up here and how I managed to make my life capsize without my being aware of it. I need to go home now, but since you have already helped me discover so many answer... I'd like to come and chat with you again, he said with a wink.

- Come anytime, my friend, I have no intention of moving. I haven't had such a beautiful place in a long time, he said smiling. And when do you intend to leave?

-Tomorrow morning. I'm going to call my wife later to tell her to come and get me. It is time that I take my life in hand, he finished with emotion in his voice.

Bruno added nothing, appreciating his courage.

The Path

<u>Renewal</u>

Jack watched through the bedroom window, as his children were getting on the bus that took them to school. Then he went down to second floor of the house he rented to go to the kitchen. Two months had passed since his return and, despite all the difficulties he had had to face, he had never regretted his choice for even a minute.

- Hello, he heard as he entered the room.
- Hello, replied Jack, approaching his wife to give her a hug.
- How are you this morning? she asked.
- Like a cat!
- Like a what?
 - Forget it. It's a personal joke, he said.
- You're going to have a lot to do today.
- Not that much after all. I just have a little to do this morning. I received a text from my lawyer that all the documents are ready and that the meeting between he and the other lawyers to finalize the separation papers is confirmed.
- How do you feel?
- Fine... surprisingly, I am now at peace with everything that has happened. The past is behind me and it only remains for us to build the future as we wish, he said, kissing her cheek.
- I can't wait for this to be over, she commented as she got closer, then we can finally move on.
- Thank you for being there for me, Jack said, taking her lovingly in his arms.

She touched his face with her hand, to answer him:

- Thank *you*... for always being there.
- Do you know what I realized this morning while watching the kids leave?
- Tell me ...
- I realized that what I will lose by going to the lawyer, he said in a serene voice, will never be worth as much as what I will gain by staying with you three.

He took the time to look at her carefully, savoring every second of her presence.

- What do you intend to do next? she asked after a moment. You won't have much to do.

A mischievous gleam shone in his eyes when he replied:

- I'm going to see a friend!

<u>Clarification</u>

- It's like in the jungle. You must have often seen this in Africa: the weakest are eaten by the strongest. Everything was taken: the house, the business, the investments, everything. Fortunately, they did not manage to touch what belonged to my wife before our marriage. It gives us some respite.

Bruno listened to Jack tell him about the events of the past few months.

- It must not have been easy...
- No, indeed, but the positive point in all this story is that I rediscovered my wife. And I must admit, in all honesty, that without her, I would not have made it. Do you know what else I realized?
- I'm listening to you.
- I thought she had changed over the years, but I was wrong. It was I who had changed without knowing it, and I don't think I would have noticed it if all that had happened would not have happened.
- We have to pay a high price sometimes to learn the truth, don't you think?
- You're right, replied Jack, taking a break to reflect. It is as if you were to buy a car that is worth a certain amount, but you end up paying double because you do not listen to anyone; you remain deaf to the messages that life sends you.

- Yep...

- What I mean by that...it's not that what I learned was not worth it, but the price is what I had to pay to understand what I needed to understand. And I should add that I am not just talking about the material side, but above all from the point of view of life itself. What I suffered and what the others had to live because of it, that is the truly high price, the rest, it can be replaced. But life? Irreplaceable...If I had discovered this before, I would have lost less in the exchange.

- What do you mean?

- That we don't have to take the most difficult paths, as I did, to understand. When things started to go downhill, I partnered with people with whom I didn't feel comfortable.

- And?

- And I did it, not because I followed my intuition, but rather because I followed what I believed were my needs...

- Which were aroused and amplified by your worries and fears, finished Bruno.

- Exactly! And, as in the jungle, the predators can smell when the prey is weakened...

-...and they become easy targets, concluded Bruno once again.

- There you go!

Sitting side by side on the steps of an old stone staircase that seemed to lead nowhere, Bruno and Jack watched two squirrels run after each other.

- They have no problems, commented Jack, pointing to the two small animals.

- Hey, are you doing biology now?

- Well, aren't you funny? replied Jack, amused by the reply. But it's still true, look at them, they have no problems.

- You think? Why do you believe that is?

- ...?

- If we were squirrels, if we thought, lived, felt like them, maybe we would have squirrel... problems?

Jack was not sure if he understood the words.

- It is only a question of perception, explained Bruno, they perceive life as they are. How do you see your life?

- What do you mean?...

- Do you perceive your life as it is? Or as it is not, compared to what you would like it to be?

- You lost me there...Could you tell me what you want, in a way that doesn't require me to read an instruction manual?

- Look, said Bruno laughing, while rummaging in his pockets to get out a pencil and a piece of paper.

- You want to draw something?

- No, he said still laughing, writing on the piece of paper. Here, go to this address, ask for Adam, and you tell him that I sent you.

- Who is it? Jack asked, taking the paper.

- Someone with whom you can continue this conversation. Trust me, you have everything to gain.

Jack looked at the paper.

Neuroscience Research Institute.

- This is what you told me about the other day, he said. Am I really so crazy as to need to go there?

Bruno laughed and replied:

- You be the judge.

The Meeting

- It must be here, Jack said aloud to himself.

After wandering around for a while trying to find the address indicated on the paper, Jack looked at what he believed was his destination. An old-fashioned style building, partitioned between two other buildings, it looked like time had begun to separate it from the others. It was not at all how he had imagined the institute. He parked his car nearby and went to ring the bell.

- Who is it? he heard on the other side of the door.
- My name is Jack.
- What do you want?
- Bruno sent me.

A silence was heard, followed by the sound of a latch being unlocked. When the door opened, Jack saw no one. He stepped inside and discovered a man in a wheelchair watching him.

- Bruno gave me your address, he said before the man's silence.
- I know, he called.
- I suppose you are Adam, said Jack, a little surprised at his reply.
- In the flesh, replied the man, rising from his chair to hold out his hand to him. Nice to meet you.
- Likewise, assured Jack, shaking his hand in complete astonishment. Can you walk?
- Of course. What is so extraordinary about that? So can you, from what I can see.
- I thought that...in your chair...
- Never trust appearances, Adam cut him off. Follow me, he said, walking towards a corridor with a sly smile on his lips.

Jack did so, curious to know who this strange character was. The end of the corridor opened onto a large room which, in turn, opens onto a sort of interior garden. Adam took his place in one of the two armchairs which framed a small pink wooden table. On the table was placed a steaming pot and two cups. Adam then invited Jack to do likewise and have a seat.

- So tell me, what is your visit worth to me? asked Adam.

- I'm not sure yet, replied Jack, doubtful of what he was doing there. I had a discussion a few days ago with Bruno, whom you know I believe, when, without further warning or explanation, he gave me your address. So here I am.

- And you came like that, without hesitation?

- Not quite, I hesitated for a long time. To tell you the truth, I was not sure what to think of his proposal.

- But that didn't stop you from coming...

- I discussed it with my wife, because I found it all a little odd, but, after reflection, we decided that it cost me nothing to come.

- And what were you talking about that was so important for Bruno to send you here? Adam asked, his manner of speaking becoming less formal.

-We were talking about perception, but I must admit that I did not have time to understand what he was trying to explain to me.

- Aahh...perception, Adam repeated, settling in his chair. A great mystery for such a small word.

- ...?

- Do you know what it is? asked Adam.

- The way we interpret what is happening to us?

- That's all!

- I think so. Why? There is something else?

Adam leaned forward in his chair before answering:

It was not a question, he said. That's all... *is* the answer.

The Butler

- Yes, and he invited me to sleep here.

Jack, on the phone, finished telling his wife about his meeting with Adam.

- He is very nice, Jack continued, I did not speak to him for a long time, but since it was getting late, he invited me to stay. According to him, it could take a while before I will be able to comprehend what I am looking for...I love you too, don't worry...yes, I will keep you posted and contact you tomorrow...without fail...Good night to you too!

When he had hung up, before going to his room, Jack went to the kitchen where, as Adam had suggested, he could eat a little something if he wished.

- Good evening, sir, he heard behind him once in the room.
- Good evening, replied Jack, turning to find a woman busy pulling ingredients from a cupboard.
- My name is Monique, she introduced herself. Is there anything I can do for you?
- Uh...well...no, well, I don't think so. My name is Jack, he said, stepping forward to reach out to him. Nice to meet you.

It's a sort of butler...woman, he said to himself, scrutinizing her. He had not expected to meet a servant on duty at this late hour.

- Can I help you with something?
- Not really, he replied, Adam told me that if I was hungry, I could come and have a bite to eat here.

- No problem, she replied, I can prepare a little something for you, if you want.
- Oh no worries, I can manage, thank you anyway.

Jack looked at the woman, had not budged an inch.

- Well, if you want, he said suddenly uncomfortable, a tomato sandwich will do.
- With pleasure, replied the woman with a smile. Would you like the bread toasted?
- Uh...Yes I would.
- With cheese?
- ...Yes...
- Butter or mayonnaise?
- Mayo...

Jack wanted to add 'sliced diagonally' while he watched Monique go to the fridge, but held back.

- And sliced diagonally, of course, he heard her say quietly.

Astonished, Jack asked her:

- Why did you just say that?
- Well, because it's the correct way to slice sandwiches, really... don't you agree?

- Yes, of course... confirmed Jack embarrassed. Have you been working for Adam for a long time? he continued, just trying to make conversation.
- I don't work for Adam, she said, turning to face him.
- I thought that...
- Adam and I help each other in various tasks.
- And have you and Adam been helping you in various tasks for a long time?
- Several years, replied Monique, continuing to prepare the sandwich. Adam is a pretty unpredictable man, you know.

- I noticed. And how did you meet him? I hope that wasn't indiscreet.

- No worries. We met when we were both attending the same university.

Monique placed the sandwich on the table and then sat down.

- How about you? Why are you here?

- As I explained to Adam, I am going through difficult times. I was talking with a mutual friend and we got onto the subject of perception, which led me here.

- Oh, and what would you like to know about perception?

- What it is exactly.

- Hmm ... If you'll permit me, I'd say that it is what you make of it, replied Monique, in a completely natural tone.

Jack looked at her for a moment before continuing…

- What do you mean?

- That it is you who create the perception of what you want.

- I don't understand.

- It is simple really, but I don't want to annoy you with my personal opinions.

- You don't bother me at all. I am open to anything that can bring me a new point of view.

- Alright, in that case, here is mine. All life events are neutral, always... neutral. They have no basic meaning other than what you give them. The perception you have of things comes from yourself, according to your life experience, your expectations, your understanding, your interpretation, your needs, etc. Events, situations, people, things, everything is neutral. And each person will perceive differently, according to themselves.

- Wait, replied Jack, you are trying to tell me that everything that I have lived in my life so far, I have lived because I perceived it as it happened?

- Not exactly, it's actually the opposite. Things happened as you perceived them.

Jack continued to watch Monique, trying to make sense of the ideas which were jostling around in his head.

- Besides, she went on, that's what you're doing right now.
- Sorry?
- Let me try to be more clear, and of course, this is all just my opinion. What you perceive at each moment and what you interpret is your own creation, but it is often in relation to what you have as expectations or as hopes, essentially, the things that you want. What you imagine about what may happen in the future or what has happened in the past does not exist in reality. Nothing has any control over you, other than what you believe to be or what could be true.

Jack listened attentively, trying to take in the information.

- Everything always happens in the present moment, she continued, even what you apprehend, whether negative or positive. Likewise if something that has happened in your past, long ago or recently, is still present in your life, it is because you are seeking it in your memories, and in doing so, you bring it into your present, accompanied by the perception that you had in this same past, but which, in reality, no longer exists. But as you recreate in the present a perception of a past moment, you have the feeling that it is always present, but it is false.

Jack wondered what on earth was going on and especially what her words were supposed to mean. Being in contact with a man like Adam had quite surprising side effects, he thought before continuing:

- Thank you very much, he said looking at his yet uneaten sandwich, but I think I'll use the rest of the night to digest everything you've said.
- No problem, replied Monique, getting up, see you tomorrow then?
- Yes, with pleasure, said Jack, picking up his cold sandwich and taking it to his room.

<u>Who is Telling the Truth?</u>

When Jack presented himself the next morning in the dining room, Adam, who was already there, received him in a friendly manner.

- Did you sleep well? he asked.
- More or less. My brain took time to calm down after I met Monique last night.
- It doesn't surprise me, said Adam, amused, it's a fairly common reaction among people who have the pleasure of chatting with her.
- Hello! they both heard, when Monique came in turn to come and sit with Jack.

The latter was surprised by her action, but made no comment.

- And what would you like to eat this morning? Adam asked for Jack. Potatoes, eggs, cereal?
- Cereal will be fine.
- Same for me, said Monique in her turn.
- All right, cereal for everyone then, Adam replied cheerfully, heading for the kitchen.

Jack watched him go, then looked towards Monique who was smiling.

- Is something wrong? she asked him.
- I think I'm missing something...
- Ah well, what then?
- Shouldn't you be in the kitchen and Adam here?
- Why?

- Well... Jack hesitated, I wouldn't want to sound rude, but shouldn't the staff be in the kitchen preparing breakfast at the moment?

- Yes, of course, that's what's going on, right?

Jack stared at Monique, perplexed.

- Why is Adam in the kitchen?
- Because he is the butler and as you just pointed out, his place is there...at the moment.
- But who are you then?
- Monique...you remember? We talked last night...
- Yes...but I thought that...
- I was the servant?
- Yes...Something like that, replied Jack suddenly embarrassed.

Monique displayed a bright smile, before continuing:

- Bad perception... or am I wrong? she said.

Jack was still staring at her, understanding less and less.

- As I said before, I think something is missing, he said.
- I think I owe you an explanation then...
- That would be nice, because I admit that I'm a bit lost.

Monique poured coffee into their respective cups, and began:

- So here you are...I am Monique Paradis, Doctor of Neurosciences, and Adam is Adam, my butler. When our mutual friend Bruno called me to let me know that someone was coming to see me, he also explained the reason.
- So you knew I would come?
- Yes, and I confess that it is not the first time that Bruno has asked me for this service.
- To receive someone?
- Right.
- But why did he tell me to ask for Adam?

- This is what we had agreed upon for your arrival.

- But you and Adam did not meet at University then?

- Of course we did. I was a student and Adam worked there as a maintenance worker. For no particular reason, we immediately had affinities and I promised him that if one day I became rich, I would hire him. That's what I did as soon as I could. But rest assured, he is not the only one to take care of the house.

- What about Bruno?

- I was his teacher when he came back from Africa and went back to school. He had gone through hard times and I helped him find... let's call it... the path he was looking for. He and I, we immediately got along.

Jack settled into his seat, sorting in his mind what had just happened.

- But why put on this act?

- So that you can understand...

- What?

Monique came closer, and, with a mischievous air, said to him in a low voice:

- What perception truly is... don't you see?

<u>Putting Things into Place</u>

Jack and Monique, joined by Adam, had finished their breakfast and were chatting.

- Do you mind if I speak informally with you? said Monique to Jack.
- No problem. It's okay with me.
- Very well, then I will continue. Unlike experience, words are not very good teachers. Perception comes in part from what we desire, from our expectations, from what we hope for in life. For example, coming here, what did you expect?
- To meet a man who could help me find the answers to what I was looking for.
- And what did you find when you arrived?
- A man whom I found rather strange, but whose name was Adam as Bruno had told me.
- And what did Bruno tell you about Adam?
- Uh... nothing!
- And you thought when meeting him that he was the right person to help you find out what you wanted?
- Yes, indeed.
- Yet nothing indicated to you that it was.
- No, it was even quite the opposite.
- However, continued Monique, you still perceived it as being that way.
- Right.
- And when did you meet me in the kitchen? What indicated to you that I could be the servant?
- In reality... nothing, replied Jack after a moment of reflection.
- But?

- Your pleasant attitude, your proposal to prepare a sandwich for me, the place where you were, the fact that, for me, I had already met the person I came to see, you could only be the servant...

Monique looked at him carefully, then continued:

- So, if I understood correctly, you perceived us both according to what you hoped or what you logically believed that it could or should be.
-Sort of, well... actually yes, that's pretty much it... he realized.
- Now tell me, during the negative past experiences that led you to lose what you had worked so hard to build, as you told me earlier, could you have acted like that?
- I don't understand...
- The perception you had of the two of us was based on the need you felt to find an answer, right?
- Ok, so?
- Do you agree that a need is an emotion that you feel?
- Yes.
- And that the need you felt could have influenced the perception of what you experienced when arriving here?
- Yeah.
- And that need and fear are two emotions?
- Indeed...
- So here is my point: if you perceived events in your past based on the emotion that you felt, let's say fear in this case, and that what you lived was interpreted and filtered by this feeling, is it possible that you based your actions on an interpretation that was in fact... false?

Jack looked at Monique and Adam in turn, trying to sort through and organize in his mind the things he had just heard.

The Example

- We act according to our expectations, what we hope for, not what we want.

Jack told his wife about his meeting with Monique and Adam.

- She told me that perception is multifaceted. We simply feel, and if we trust ourselves enough to differentiate between our expectations, that is to say what we hope for, and what we want, then we can recognize more quickly what is good or not for us.

Diane was not sure if she fully understood what her husband was saying.

- You're looking at me as if I was speaking a foreign language... he protested.
- A little, yeah.
- It's not very clear, is it?
- Not really. Can you try to simplify?
- Okay, said Jack, taking the time to gather his thoughts. When things started to get bad, I started to get scared. I was afraid that things would stop going well, that we would lose what we had, fear of not being good enough, fear of...
- Good enough for what? Diane cut him off.
- Good enough for what I thought I should be in your eyes, said Jack with a slight tremor in his voice.
- Poor darling, she whispered, upset by the revelation, no one ever expected that from you...
- I know now, but at the time... no.

They both looked at each other in silence for a few seconds, before Jack resumed:

- I remember very well the first time I met the representative of the group who got hold of the company. I immediately felt uneasy... but I did not listen to myself, the fear that everything would get worse would take up so much space in my thoughts that I was ready to do anything to make it disappear and the means in which I believed was what he proposed to me... and it fit perfectly with the solution that I hoped for and not with the one that I really wanted. Because, as you surely know, I never wanted a partner, but I was much more in tune with what I wanted it to bring me, than I was with the bad feelings that I felt.

Jack paused, an expression of bitterness on his face. Diane looked at him, respecting the silence they shared.

- I'm so sorry, he went on, I really wanted to avoid all of this.
- It's a thing of the past now, replied Diane in a soft voice, what is done is finished. What we have in front of us, what we can build, that is what matters. The rest no longer matters to me.

She took her husband's head in her hands and said to him, eyes shining with tenderness:

- And that how; I, perceive things!

<u>Trust</u>

-Finding confidence in myself is what I find the hardest these days.

Jack was sitting cross- legged as he shared the breakfast with Bruno he had picked up at the restaurant on the way.

- What do you mean?
- Feeling like I'm the only one that believes.
- Believes in what?
- In what I do, what I want. Believing that what I want is possible, achievable, believing that I am still capable of it, that I am up to it, that I will not fall back... at the end of the day, it's all this that I struggle with.

Bruno looked at Jack, took one of the sandwiches that they were eating for breakfast, opened it up and placed the ingredients, pell-mell, on the plate in front of him, and then asked:

- Can you make this sandwich again, please?

Jack looked at him, astonished, not understanding his gesture.

- What?
- I'm asking you to remake this sandwich the way it was. That's all, I'll explain after.
- Why? You didn't like how it was made?

- Stop joking around. Come on, put it together again the way it was.

Jack did so, putting back all the ingredients between the two slices of bread, then handing it to Bruno.

- Here you go! he said, curious to know what would happen next.
- But it's not the same as before, protested Bruno after examining the work.
- Obviously, it would be quite difficult for it to be identical. All the ingredients are a bit mixed up, and aren't in the same order, but everything is there, I didn't leave anything out.
- But it is not the same as before, Bruno protested, looking at what he had in his hands. I would have liked you to give me this sandwich as it was before.
- But it's impossible, come on... I'm surprised you don't understand this. There's no way to put everything back in exactly the same way. The ingredients are all mixed up, but everything is there. If you taste it, you will see, it is the same sandwich, same taste, same texture. If you close your eyes, you won't be able to tell the difference.
- You want to make me believe that if I look at this sandwich, even if I see it totally different when compared to how it was before, it is the same?
- Exactly, but what do you not understand about that?

Bruno stared at Jack without saying a word; Jack glanced at Bruno and then the sandwich, waiting for a response, when suddenly… He realized…

- I think I understand... he declared.
- What?
- That I'm like this sandwich…
- That is to say?

- That I am the same as before, with all that I was, and even more. But... at the same time different by the experience that I lived and, that all my ingredients, that is to say what I am, are now placed differently, but... that I'm still the same, and maybe even a little bit improved.

Bruno, smiling in satisfaction, took the time to lean back before answering:

- What you believe... becomes, he said teasingly.

The Garden

You are the children of the universe.
What you believe, will be.

- Goodness, it's almost harassment, Jack said aloud to himself.
- It makes you think, doesn't it?

Jack, who had stopped to read a note written on a small board in the public garden he was visiting, turned around. The man who had just spoken looked at him smiling, with a peaceful air.

- Yes, indeed, replied Jack, returning his smile.
- It took me a long time to understand it, said the stranger, and even more to be able to write it.

Intrigued, Jack looked at the man without saying anything, who said:

- But let me introduce myself. My name is Benoit, he said, holding out his hand. And you are?
- Jack, replied the latter, taking the man's hand in his. Did you write this note?
- Yes, as well as all the others.
- You work here then?
- You could say that, yes. The whole garden belongs to me as well as the surrounding land.
- Oh, I thought it was a public space.
- It is, I have built these places over the years and everyone can come at their leisure.

Jack glanced around and realized that the landscaping made it look more like a garden worthy of the Palace of Versailles than a simple public park.

- You have good taste, he said, and you're very generous to agree to share such a magnificent place.
- It's natural. When you receive, you give back, it's my way of giving back to the community. But don't get me wrong, it's a dream come true: I feel an immense pleasure in watching all these people enjoy and appreciate this space.
- You're lucky.
- Lucky how?
- To have been able to realize your dream.

Benoit looked at him for a moment without a word, before answering:

- Luck has nothing to do with it. It is mostly because I believed in it. But I admit that it was not always as easy as it seems. I had to restart some phases multiple times and often in the forty years that it took me, I doubted my ability to succeed.
- Can I ask you why? If you don't mind...
- Of course, he replied, pointing to one of the many benches in the garden, but why don't we sit in the shade? We will be much more comfortable. At my age, it is better to avoid exposure to the sun; it is not good for my health.

Following him, Jack noted that the man did indeed appear very old.

- If it's not too intrusive, can I ask you your age?
- No, it isn't, reassured Benoit. I'm just starting my ninety-first year, and I still have lots of projects to accomplish. Here, we'll be fine here, he said, settling down on a bench.
- Have you ever, during all these years, believed in something and, despite everything you do, it seems like you always get the same result? Jack asked, taking his place next to him.

Too often for my taste, said Benoit with a grimace. It took me a long time to understand why, and but it turned out that the reason was very simple.

- Oh really?

- It's fascinating to realize that some things are so simple that we miss them.

- What do you mean by that?

- That sometimes the solution to what we are looking for is so obvious that we don't even consider it. *It cannot be just that,* we say to ourselves, and yet...

- I don't understand, said Jack.

- Your question, for example...

Benoit told Jack, then paused as if he were pondering something special... before continuing:

- About doing something in every way possible to always achieve the same result ...

- Yes?

- Tell me, how do you react when something like this happens in your life? When you try to do something, in every possible way you can imagine, and the end result is always the same...What do you do?

- Well... I do what I can, really believing in it, wanting it, and after a while I see the result and try to find out why nothing has changed.

- And how do you do that?

- I don't see what you're getting at.

- You're getting there, replied Benoit, so... what do you do?

- I examine what didn't work, what I could have done differently, what I did badly, and then...

- And you focus on what didn't work?

- Of course, to make sure I don't do it again. Isn't that better?

- No.

- No? Explain to me, because I'm getting lost...

- When you focus on what is wrong, you can only reproduce what you've given your attention to.

Benoit looked at Jack again with that funny look...

- Are you able to walk in one direction for a long time, keeping your head turned behind you?
- Uh... no.
- When you stumble over an obstacle and get up again, do you stay there looking at the obstacle or do you resume your path, immediately forgetting it?
- I resume my journey, forgetting it immediately...
- When you go to the buffet of a restaurant to fill your plate, once you've sat back down to eat, do you constantly look back to see what you did not choose?
- No.
- Why?
- Because I don't want it, replied Jack immediately.
- And?
- It is useless to focus on what I do not want, and because it is a waste of my time not to appreciate what I have... concluded Jack, realizing the importance of what he was saying.
- And can you be looking at what you want and what you don't want at the same time?
- No, of course not. As soon as I focus on one thing, the other disappears from my view, he agreed, more and more aware of his words.
- What should you do then?
- I have to make a choice... prioritizing what I want and stick to it, replied Jack, leaning back as if he had just had a revelation.

Benoît looked at him for a moment before continuing:

- It's simple, isn't it?

After a moment of reflection, Jack said looking at him:

- Almost too simple!

<u>**Comprehension**</u>

- The way I see life is very different now.

Jack and his wife were quietly enjoying the backyard of their rental house while sharing a good bottle of sparkling wine.

- You know what? he continued. Even if we had a yard ten times larger in the other house, I do not remember feeling as good as I do in this one.
- I fully understand how you feel, Diane exclaimed, raising her cup.

She took a sip, then returned to the conversation Jack had had with Benoit.

- And what else did he tell you?
- In reality, it is much more what I understood for myself rather than the words he said. We talked about all kinds of things; he told me the story of his garden and a lot of other stuff, but what struck me the most about this meeting and what I will remember is this: we have to re-learn how to think.
- What do you mean?
- Listen carefully, and you can correct me if you think I'm wrong.
- Okay.
- Let's take the example of a participant in a mountain running race. He follows a direction and often he will have to cross obstacles, like streams, fallen trees, rocks bigger than him, etc. If he trips, how does he react?
- He gets up and continues?

- Right! But mainly, he will not be interested in what made him trip or why. He already understood why: he didn't jump high enough, his stride was too short, whatever, only one thing matters... where he is going!

- The rest is already understood and there is no longer any reason to pay attention to it, is that it?

- Right! But too often, we stop at what makes us stumble and try to dissect everything to understand why. Because of this, we stop our progress and start going in circles, instead of just learning from the experience and moving on. And from there, we get stuck in what we did wrong and perpetuate it indefinitely... as I did myself...

- And why would you do that?

- Because that's what I was taught to do: look at what is not working to find a solution. Hence the importance of re-educating one's way of thinking.

- And how can we actually do that? asked Diane.

- Being aware of it, to start with.

- Then what?

Jack looked deeply into her eyes before answering:

- I don't know yet, but I feel that I will soon find out...

<u>**We**</u>

- She comes to speak for free once a month for anyone who wants to attend.

Bruno explained to Jack who the little woman was who had taken the stage at the front of the room. They were there for the monthly conference, offered by a homeless assistance center.

- She helps a lot of people in need, he continued, whispering. She is a survivor of the Vietnam war refugee camp, one of the *Boat People.* She has quite the life story.
    - And why did you bring me here?
    - Because you asked questions, replied Bruno.
    - And is this my answer?
    - Maybe she and many others. Answers are given to you all the time, but do you understand them? That is the real question!
    - Let's hope she has good answers then...

The reply amused Bruno.

- And by the way, which question in particular am I supposed to find answers to? Which one, among the dozens of dozen questions I have been able to ask? Asked Jack, popping up like a jack-in-the-box.
    - Hush, said Bruno, inviting him to lower his voice. You will recognize the question by hearing the answer. Listen, he finished, turning to listen to the speaker who had started to speak.

She was a young Asian girl in her forties, without any accent to her speech, Jack told himself that she must have arrived in the country quite young.

- Every event we experience, without exception, she said, is in itself neutral. The same event experienced by one person will be perceived differently by another person. The event itself has no meaning of its own. It has certainly happened to you to witness something with other people, and afterwards, when you talk about the event, you realize that everyone presents the facts differently. Each witness tells the same story that you tell, but from another point of view, the point of view stemming from one's own perception. It is the same for our life.

The crowd nodded in agreement, confirming what she had said. Jack listened, surprised by the speech which seemed very similar to the one Monique had given him.

- Everything in our life starts from us, she continued, we are all the center of the universe... in our own life of course, clarified the young woman with a smile at the audience. We are the center of *our* universe, of *our* world, of *our* life. We are the only ones capable of deciding that we are ready to give in or to succeed, and even if we are influenced by so many external factors, the only person who really has the final say in what happens to us... is ourselves. We are all capable to take back this privilege, too often overlooked, that we have always had. It is up to us to start, just a little, just a small action, without anyone knowing, just to see, just in case... But, she continued, looking at the crowd as if she wanted to ensure her words would penetrate her audience's minds, we also have the right not to make this decision. And that is called... free will.

A silence so silent that you could almost hear it, reigned in the room. Everyone waited eagerly for her to continue, and Jack, who looked from the woman to the crowd and then from the crowd to the woman, could nearly make out a common sentiment emanating from all of these people who listened to her almost religiously. It was a feeling which seemed to float in the air, a feeling he easily recognized, because it was one he had been feeling for a long time... a feeling of hope!

__Interpretation__

- Congratulations, I think you were able to inspire a lot of people once again.

Bruno was shaking the hand of the speaker. He and Jack had joined her behind the scenes after the conference.

- Thank you, that's very nice, she said.
- Let me introduce you to Jack, Bruno continued pointing to him, this is the friend I told you about on the phone, Jack this is Nad.
- Pleased to meet you, she said, holding out her hand to Jack, who was surprised by what Bruno had said about the phone call.
- So am I, he said, taking her outstretched hand. Congratulations. I very much appreciated your speech, especially when you talked about how we interpret the events that occur in our lives, that part particularly troubled me.
- Oh really? And why is that?
- I don't want to take up your time. After a conference like this, you surely need some rest.
- Quite the contrary, the woman said laughing, I always come out of these conferences feeling super energized, so humor me; tell me what you thought. I assure you that I will enjoy exchanging with you on the subject just as much as you, and maybe even more. But please, first have a seat, she said, pointing to the chairs near her.
- Thank you, replied Jack as he took his seat next to Bruno. You said that no matter what we are going through, the events we experiences are always neutral. They have no meaning except for the meaning we give to them.
-Yes, that's correct.
- I have really been trying to understand that, but when I look at certain moments in my life, there are periods that do not fit what you are describing.

- May I speak freely with you?
- Yes, of course.
- Okay then, can you be more specific?

Jack looked at Bruno, unsure whether or not to continue.

- Go ahead, his friend said encouragingly, I'm sure Nad is impatient to know about your experiences.
- Absolutely, she said, I surely learn as much from the experiences of people I meet as they do from the experiences I share, so speak openly.
- Okay, said Jack. So here it is: I lived some events not too long ago during which I lost everything that I had managed to build throughout my life.

Jack reflected for a moment, trying to find the right words.

- There are certain moments during which I was able to give my 'personal interpretations,' but when a bailiff comes knocking at your door without warning to tell you that you are no longer at home, when it is indeed your home, to tell you that nothing inside is yours anymore, to confiscate your cars right before your eyes, no matter how hard I try, I can't come up with any interpretation besides: "I have nothing left, and my family is on the street."

Jack looked at Nad while waiting for an answer. Bruno wanted to speak, but she waved him off.

- First, I understand very well what you have just expressed, she replied in a calm voice, and even if that will not change anything that happened, I want to tell you that I sympathize with you. On the other hand, if you don't mind, I would like to give you my point of view about what you have just told me.

Jack felt a feeling of tranquility invade him. Was it the sound of her voice, the serenity she displayed? He wasn't sure, but he nodded at her request.

- First, she began, I fully agree with you. In the situation you mentioned, I would surely have reacted in the same way. Nor do I see other interpretations to give to the situation. But if I understood correctly, what you tell me seems to me rather to be an outcome, than an event in itself.

- What do you mean?

- That in all the events that preceded what you described, you made choices. You made decisions about what was going on in your life, based on the interpretation that you made of it, you were led to make other decisions that you thought were the right ones. I do not know your life, but I am convinced that if we analyze it together, and be certain that my goal is not to hurt you at all, you would be surprised to find that what happened to you comes largely from yourself, without you being aware of it.

Nad fell silent, watching Jack, who did not say a word.

- Excuse me if I seem insensitive to what you have experienced, I assure you my intentions are quite the opposite. On the other hand, if you want, we can resume our discussion at another time and go over it together.

Jack cast a discreet glance at Bruno before looking at her again and answering:

- Okay...I would like that!

Result

- I made a poor choice and associated with the wrong people, it's as simple as that.

Jack, who had joined Nad in a cafe a week after their first meeting, was telling his story.

- Everything fell apart because of this affair, he explained. They invested in a shady business and it went bad. Since my company was linked to theirs by the contract I had just signed, it was included in the legal proceedings which led to what I've already told you about. They took everything.
- And you had no recourse?
- No. In any case, I no longer had the means to do anything. Everything I owned was seized, even the squirrels in the backyard were afraid of having their acorns stolen, he quipped. I could no longer pay anything, let alone lawyers who demanded expensive fees before they would even look at the case. I'm sure that now you can understand why I am a little resistant to some of your statements.
- Yes, I understand. It's my turn now to explain my point of view, and you can decide afterwards, okay?
- Okay, I'm listening.
- First a question: the feeling you experienced of having lost everything, is it from a material or emotional point of view?
- I don't understand...
- Is it the monetary value or the sentimental value of what you lost that is important to you?

Jack leaned back in his chair to think. He had not yet considered the situation from this angle.

- In my heart, he replied after a while, it was all that I had built, my reason for living, my dream come true...

Without a word, Nad gestured for him to continue.

- It was also my future, I saw myself aging as the head of this company. It would have allowed me to do whatever I wanted. You understand, all my past and my future disappeared at the same time...

A silence came over them that Nad did not interrupt, watching him with respect.

- Wow, exclaimed Jack after a moment, that is quite a revelation...
- Surprised?
- A little yes, especially that it affects me this much.
- And do you find this abnormal?
- Let's say... unexpected. Despite the many moments of discouragement I went through, I had not stopped to realize the importance - from an existential point of view - of all this. I was too caught up in the whirlwind of life seeking solutions... of self-pity!
- You don't need to be so hard on yourself.
- I am simply aware. If I can recognize my strengths, I can also recognize my weaknesses. I am beginning to understand that in everything I have experienced, I was much too focused on what was wrong, on fears of what could happen and what made me make bad decisions. I also understand that by always looking at my problems, I no longer saw what was good in my life... and I walked away from it. I am not hard on myself, I am honest.
- And why do you believe you did all that?

Jack looked at her for a moment, surprised at his question.

- I don't understand...

- Why did you work so hard to have this big business. Why did you spend all this time away from those you loved in favor of this apparent success?

- To make my family happy, of course... He replied in a somewhat defensive tone.

- And did you find that happiness?

- No, of course not, you know the result ...

- But do you know what it is?

- Know what *what* is? asked Jack, somewhat annoyed by her questions.

- Happiness... do you know what it is?

Jack looked at the woman, who stared back at him with a steady look.

- I... have no answer, he admitted after a moment, looking away. It's funny, isn't it? I thought I had done everything to reach it and I can't even tell you what it is.

It's hard to discover what we don't know, said Nad, after a moment's silence.

- Indeed... And what do you think happiness is? Bruno told me that you had a childhood that was, shall we say... different?

- You could say that, yes. The first years of my life were lived in refugee camps in Indochina after the war in Vietnam, then there was immigration and everything that goes with it: adaptation, integrating into a new culture, trying to find acceptance, etc. I have indeed a personal vision of what happiness is. For me, it is above all... to appreciate life, savor each passing moment in order to recognize its importance. Happiness is unique to everyone; it is to see life through a child's eyes: with simplicity and without judgment.

- It must have been difficult for you, this adaptation…

- The most amazing thing is that I remember so many moments of happiness at the camp. We were united and shared what little we had. We sang on the guitar around a fire in the evening. I was only four years old, and yet I can easily feel and relive the experience just by thinking about it. Perhaps it is because of the conditions I survived when I was young that makes me perceive happiness as a state. But you too, with what you have experienced in recent months, experienced this condition of survival in your own way.

- Is that why it has become so important for me to be happy?

- Perhaps. Happiness is significantly more accessible to a person in survival mode than to a person living in a world of excess.

- As I was, continued Jack.

- Yes, as you were, Nad confirmed. And now?

- Now... I have taken notes in here, he said, pointing to his head, that if I want a better life, I must appreciate what I already have, and only from there can find what I want... if I really want it.

- Is that all?

- And also that what I have discovered that what I have lived so far may not have been the easiest way, but at the same time I know that what I have succeeded and what I have learned about myself, I can no longer ignore it .

- Do you mean that your perception and your interpretation of what you went through, as difficult as it may have been, has changed?

Jack looked her straight in the eyes and, without hesitation, replied:

- Absolutely!

The Quay

- It makes sense, doesn't it?

Jack dangled his feet in the water, admiring the landscape that lay before him while sitting on the quay that Bruno had brought them to.

- And why does it take us so long to understand? he asked in reply to his friend, with whom he was exchanging about their meeting with Nad.
- Education, answered Bruno, we are all educated to act according to rules established by society. Religions: which were conceived by the man by to make him believe that his capacity to create his life as he wanted it depended on the good will of a God which they made in their images. Our economic model: which sends us the message that happiness comes from the outside, in what you own, what you look like, what you do better than your neighbor, from comparison. In short, of everything that makes our world, such a unique world.
- It's distressing, said Jack, almost sadly.
- Not that much, no!
- What? After what you have just described, do you still think that the world is beautiful?
- Of course, because what I just described is only part of this world.
- And what is the other part?
- The one you want.
- What do you mean?
- What if you told me?

Bruno stared at him defiantly, which made Jack want to take his challenge.

- Okay. In your speech, you forgot to mention the people who come to the aid of those who need it... as you do!
- OK...
- You also forgot to mention all the organizations which, in spite of what people may say, really do help the poor and people with diseases.
- Go on...
- There are also those who come together to help during major disasters, and you did not mention either, the movements and new forms of awareness that are appearing more and more which support what, you, Nad and others have been telling me.
- All right, is there anything else?
- The world is full of good and generous people and, believe me, I speak from experience, specified Jack, because I have met several lately. I would add that my experience was neither good nor bad, it just was, that's all. The world is not only dark, O, Great Sage of the Street... it is also full of light, and it is up to us to choose in which part we want to live.

Jack finished speaking, a little surprised at himself by what he had said. Bruno looked at him for a moment, and finally said to him, displaying a broad smile:

- I think you don't need me anymore!

The Arrival

<u>**Homecoming**</u>

The years had passed, dotted with obstacles and successes. Sitting on the lawn, Jack looked ahead of him, lost in thought…

- Eight years, he said aloud to himself. Eight years have already passed and there are days when I feel that I have understood nothing.
- ...
- You could at least say something, he said after a moment.
- It's true, he heard Bruno answer.
- And there are days, it is the opposite, I have the impression that I have understood everything.
- It's also true.
- You are not very helpful today!
- It is you who decide, it is only you who have the power to decide what is true or not in your life... Unless you leave that power to someone else...
- Yes, but there are more difficult days than others.
- That too, it's always you who decides.

Jack turned to look at the stone in front of him.

- You make me sweat sometimes, you know that? With your answers full of...
- And yet, for all this time, you keep coming back to see me anyway.
- Yep, it's been so many years now... So many years that I seem to be talking to myself.
- Well then, who answers you?

Jack looked again at the tombstone in front of him…

- But you're dead, Bruno... you have been for eight years!
- I can't be that dead, at least to you, since we talk every time you want.

Jack was still looking at the stone in front of him…

- How do I know that it's not just my imagination?
- It is you who decide!
- Yeah, yeah...

Jack could easily imagine Bruno looking at him, with his eternal smile waiting for his answer.

- But even still, it's not up to me to decide if you are alive or not, is it?
- Of course it is. And you can also decide what you believe, and whether what you live is real or not, and whether, for you, I am alive or not. Whatever you decide, it will be your truth, therefore your reality.
- ...?
- Death is just an illusion, Jack, remember. When people suffer from someone's disappearance, it is often because they let them die in their hearts, and what they believe becomes real... for them. We are always in connection with the people we love and who love us, living on this planet or not, and this even if we do not see them. It is as if they had left for a long trip to a foreign country.
- That is to say?
- Have you ever had someone you love going on a trip for several months?
- Yes, of course.
- And how did you feel?
- Fine.
- You weren't crying, weren't sad?
- Well no, I was even happy for her, why this question?

- However, the person was absent, you could no longer see him, hear him, touch him. You didn't even know if she had had a good trip or even if you would see her again one day, and yet...

- Okay, I get it. Even if I didn't see her physically anymore, she still existed in a certain way.

- In your life, Bruno confirmed.

-If I believe it, continued Jack.

- What you believe becomes your...

- Hello, Mister! interrupted a child's voice.

Jack turned back in surprise, having believed himself to be alone, to see a young girl aged about six, looking up at him.

- You too, are you talking with my Grandpa? asked the child.

- Your Grandpa?

- Yes, it's my Grandpa who's sleeping there, she replied pointing vaguely to a spot on the lawn. He and my dad also chat together every time we come here. I don't hear anything, she continued gesturing, but my dad says that feelings are more important than words.

- Your father is a wise man.

- I don't know... but I love him very much!

Jack, amused, looked at the child and looked again at the place she had shown him, when he heard another voice.

- Samu... don't bother the gentleman!

He turned around again and this time discovered a dark-skinned woman walking in their direction.

- Excuse me, said the lady to Jack, she has no shame.

- Oh, it's nothing. At this age, it's natural, he said while looking again at the name inscribed on the stone, wondering if it was in the right place before asking as he got up: but tell me, did she say this was her grandpa?

- Yes, indeed, but she never met him. It was her father who explained that to her. He sometimes takes her with him when he comes for a walk.

It's strange, Jack thought, murmuring in a barely audible voice as if he was talking to himself, looking at the name on the stone. In all this time that I have known him, I had never took the time to find out if he had had children. A little restrained by their meeting, he looked at the lady and the child, before asking:

- Did you come here alone?
- No, my husband is parking the car. Samu was really impatient to come, so we got out first.
- I'll leave you to be as a family then, said Jack, feeling a little confused by the situation.
- No, stay. If you are here, it is because you must certainly know Bruno too, so you do not bother us at all. And anyway, I see my husband coming, she said, looking over Jack's shoulder, stay and I'll introduce you.

Jack turned around and saw a man coming. Nearly six feet tall, long hair grouped in a bun above his head and a long beard, the young man, who must have been in his forties, looked so much like a Viking warrior... that he recognized right away.

Why

- Mom, can I have an ice cream?

The three had been chatting for a while, sitting on the terrace of a cafe.
we call this our soul
It is not too late, replied Odede, looking at her watch. Come on, let the men talk to each other and let's have a treat.
- Yay yay yay! exclaimed the little one, jumping to her feet, ready to take off.
- I'll come back to find you here in... say, 30 minutes? She asked Yo.
- I will stay right here, he replied, watching them as they walked away.

Turning around to resume his conversation with Jack, he found Jack looking at him, not saying a word.

- Well, go on, said Yo, ask me what you've been to shy to ask.
- I know I'm repeating myself, said Jack, but I'm very happy to see you again.
- Me too, even if we didn't see each other often, I thought of you regilary, without being able to explain why, really.
- But even after what you told me once a long time ago, Jack continued, I am still missing parts of your story.
- Which parts?
- The part where you returned to other humanitarian missions after our meeting, how you saw Odede again, is she the same one you had talked about regarding the walk to get water?
- Yes, that's her.

- Okay, and the way that things have worked out for you, I'm so happy for you. That woman seems extraordinary.

She's even more than that, added Yo, all smiles.

- On the other hand, what surprises me most is to find out that Bruno is your father. That is quite unexpected...

- I can understand that; I actually thought he had told you. And since we never saw each other again...

- I thought you and he, I mean the father you talked about when we met, you weren't on very good terms.

- Indeed, we weren't... until I went to Africa for the first time, as I told you.

- But did you know he was there?

- Yes.

- But how? How did he end up there? You described him as a cold businessman.

- I remember indeed, but since I never saw you again, I did not have the opportunity to tell you the rest, something I assumed he would do later, honestly.

- Well, no... So what happened?

- A few years before my first trip to Africa that I told you about, three to be more precise, Bruno lost his brother because of a brain tumor. It took barely a month between the discovery of the tumor and his death, and he took it very badly. Especially since they were both very close; they shared the same passion... money.

Jack listened in silence, fascinated to discover the rest.

- At the funeral, he was withdrawn, and our communication was already not very good. A few months later, my mother called me to tell me that he had left for a humanitarian mission somewhere in Africa through an organization that he and his brother had been funding for years.

- Amazing, said Jack.

- Yes, that's what I told myself too. My mother explained to me that the woman in charge of the organization with whom they both had a very good relationship had offered to let him to go there for a short stay, just for a change of pace.

- And he left...

- Yes, with Mom's permission, of course, but he stayed there much longer than he had originally planned, and she herself went to see him four times in the first year. The year that followed, she went there a little less often. When I went there, it had already been two years since he had been there, and we hadn't seen each other. It was my mother who told me about it, and she kept telling me that he had changed a lot, that he had learned many things, that he was no longer the person I knew.

- And you decided to go...

- Yes. I had things to deal with, and I needed to find him as much as I needed to find myself.

- And your mother waited all this time?

- Yes, but it was not too difficult for her either. It mostly helped her to understand what he was going through and to accompany him on his journey. As much there as when he returned, when he began to do what he did.

- Living on the street?

- Exactly. Upon his return, he got rid of his involvement in the business with which he was still associated and as he had amassed more money than he could spend, he started to do what he was doing when you met him.

- And your mother accepted that?

- Yeah... But he was not on the street all the time, it was his way of giving back. The loss of his brother and his journey had made him discover another meaning in his life. The rest of the time, he was with mom. They participated in all kinds of humanitarian events together while traveling.

Without ceasing to listen to him, Jack took the time to examine Yo more carefully. Some gray streaks had begun to appear in his hair, some wrinkles on his face, but it was in Yo's gaze that maturity was expressed the most. In fact, looking at him well, he realized that as he got older, he looked more and more like his father.

- And you, Jack asked, what are you doing now?

- I divide my time between my family here and the family of Odede in Africa. It is a beautiful compromise that we both accepted. We are very active in the foundation which Bruno founded before leaving us and which my mother - by the way - directs with a master's hand.

Yo took a few seconds to observe Jack.

- But what about your life now? It can't be too bad, judging by your clothes... which are much prettier than the ones you wore the last time I saw you, he added laughing.
- It wasn't hard to do, said Jack, laughing with him. But if you have time I can tell you, he said, seeing the girls who had come skipping back from the ice cream stand.
- Don't worry, Yo replied, looking in turn towards the girls, we have all the time we need.

<u>**Example**</u>

- She seems to be having a lot of fun!

Jack and Yo were enjoying the ice cream that Odede had brought back for them while they observed the girls playing on the playground.

- It always amazes me to see her have so much fun with nothing. There are times when I think she's the younger of the two, Yo said speaking of Odede.
- It is special indeed, added Jack.
- I really have no idea where her love of life comes from, every day I learn something in her presence, just by watching her.
- She is very inspiring indeed, said Jack, everything seems so simple when I see her.

He watched as the girls finished their games and came back to them, wondering what she understood that he still hadn't grasped... just like the birds from long ago.

<u>What is Lacking</u>

- But you... tell me about you!

Now all four of them sat on the park lawn; they were chatting while keeping an eye on Samu, who slept peacefully on a blanket.

- Things gradually fit into place, explained Jack. I set up a new business, smaller and less demanding, the children continue their studies and are doing well, my wife is still as wonderful and...
- And? Yo asked, after a silence perhaps a little too long.
- And? repeated Jack, looking at a group of teenagers having fun nearby. Despite all that I have learned, understood, changed, experienced, achieved, succeeded... I feel that I am still missing something, and that's what I mean by *'and'*!

Silence ensued, but not an uncomfortable silence, just silence... until Odede broke it when she said:

- I once read about something similar in a book, she began. One of the characters asked himself this question: What do I lack? He asked himself this question because, despite his efforts to find the happiness he hoped for, he had the feeling that he was still missing something. I'm going to give you the same answer he received from a Sage, because this answer made me think and maybe it can help you too.

Jack looked at Odede, waiting attentively for the rest.

- The Sage replied: "What you lack is… yourself!"

Jack looked at her, taken aback by the response which he had never before thought of.

- Myself? he said after a few seconds, what I lack is myself? he repeated in a barely audible voice as if lost in thought.

Yo made like he wanted to speak, but Odede gestured for him to keep quiet, giving Jack the time he needed.

- What do you mean? How can you lack yourself? Every day, I try to do the best I can.
- I don't doubt it, said Odede, but to do your best and be yourself, I mean living according to your true nature, what you feel to be true inside, what you "know" to be true from within, what we call, *our soul,* this is different.
- What do you mean?
- Do you know who you really are? asked Odede, who is the Jack inside you?
- I'm starting to think I don't, he replied pensively. And you, have you managed to discover who you really are?
- Of course.
- But how?
- By becoming aware of what drives me, what makes me vibrate inside, what I believe in, what I know have always been, without being able to let it be... By giving me permission to be other than what I was taught. By daring to believe that I could be the impossible... contrary to the opinion of some.

Jack looked at her, immersed in the energy she gave off.

- I would love to be able to discover myself, he said to himself softly.
- But you already know all this, replied Odede, you may not have known it until now, but now... she finished with a huge smile, you know it!

He stared at her, searching his heart to find something…

- But how did you manage to make this change happen, he insisted, you weren't always as you are now?

- No, certainly not, especially in the environment where I grew up, she said, glancing at Yo, who listened in silence.

- So how did you start?

- With a story.

- What?

- Yes, an old story known all over the world, but told in a different way by my grandfather.

- What story?

- Do you know the story of the Scorpion and the Frog?

- Yes, of course. It's the story of a scorpion who has to cross a river and asks a frog to help him by letting climb on his golden back. But in the middle of the journey across the river, the scorpion stings the frog and says that he can't do otherwise because it's his nature, and they both sink, right?

She first glanced at Yo, then turned laughing towards Jack, to say to him:

- Not quite, I have another version...

The Story

- Do you intend to cross over?

The frog, who was watching the streams of the river intertwine, turned to see a scorpion watching it.

- What have I done to merit the honor of having you address me? she asked him, surprised that he spoke to her.
- I know it may sound unusual, but I was wondering if you intended to go to the other side?
- What if it was?
- Then I would like to ask you to take me with you, replied the scorpion, smiling.
- Well what a surprise, replied the frog. After the raging fire, she said, speaking of the bush fire that had driven all the animals to the river, a scorpion who deigns to speak to me...well fancy that!
- There aren't only bad things in life, replied the scorpion still smiling while indicating with his pincers the smoke that was approaching. We could be friends...if you'd like.
- And since when have scorpions been friends with Frogs?
- Today?... replied the scorpion, sheepishly.
- You're burning with envy... is that it?
- I couldn't have said it better myself. I recognize your great intelligence there, wheedled the scorpion.
- Blah blah blah...You can stop your false compliments. I know very well what you want.
- And you also read minds... You are more extraordinary than I thought! exclaimed the scorpion with admiration.
- Yeah...and I suppose you would like me to take you on my back, simply so that you can cross to the other side?
- Wow, what a super frog you are!

- DO YOU TAKE ME FOR A FOOL? replied the frog, raising her voice. Do you really think I'm going to take you on my back so that you can then sting me with venom?

- Uh...

- Really? Well if I am a super frog, then you are a stupid scorpion!

- Wait, no. Look, I'm not going to sting you, protested the scorpion trying to reassure her. If I stung you, we would both die, you know that. I may be a stupid scorpion, as you say, but I'm not that stupid.

- Yeah right...

- If I wanted to die crossing this river, I would have just jumped straight into the water. Since I don't know how to swim...

- Hmm, you make a good point said the frog, but still, I don't trust you.

- I assure you, insisted the scorpion, bringing his pincers together in the form of a prayer, I don't want to die any more than you do.

The frog looked at the river, then the scorpion, then the river again, knowing that if she refused, she would be condemning the scorpion to death.

- Okay, she finally answered. But I warn you, at the slightest suspicious movement, I will throw you in the water.

- I promise, said the scorpion, I will keep my stinger in the air throughout the trip.

- I'm watching you. Remember, I can see from all sides.

- No need to fear, assured the scorpion, nearly hopping with joy, ready to climb onto on her back.

<u>History (Continued)</u>

- Hey...be careful. I don't have an oxygen mask!

Hanging with its eight legs on the back of the frog, the scorpion who was doing everything possible to keep its balance, had just been involuntarily forced to swallow a large amount of water.

- Sorry, replied the frog, I had to avoid a rock, but things should be better now, the river will be calmer from here until the shore, we're almost there.
- I hope so, said the scorpion who was starting to feel an urge to...
- Hold tight, said the frog, the worst is over.
- Could you go faster? begged the scorpion, I have an uncontrollable urge to...
- You see the dead tree going sticking out of the water over there? cut the frog, that's where I'm doing to drop you off.

As soon as she got to the tree, the frog stopped and, at the precise moment that she began climbing up onto the tree, she saw out of the corner of her eye the tail of the scorpion darting towards her...

- FORGIVE ME! cried the scorpion over the roar of the river, it's too strong...
- You promised me! she cried. You...

Turning her eyes towards her passenger, what she saw left her speechless: the tail of the scorpion who was still clutching to her back, shot into a leaf of the fallen tree to empty itself of its venom.

- Aaaaaah... How good that feels! exclaimed the scorpion, pulling back so as to descend from the back of the frog. It was time!

The frog was staring at him, amazed by what she had just witnessed.

- Well, I'll be going now, and thanks for the ride, said the scorpion as soon as he landed. See you around one of these days!
- But where are you going? I thought we were friends, wondered the frog.
- Indeed, we *were*! But it's a thing of the past! You must not live in the past, it's bad for your spirit. Alright, ciao, said the scorpion, walking away, as if nothing had happened.

The frog watched him walk away, still reeling from what had just happened, when the scorpion turned back and said with a malicious air:

- And don't you dare tell anyone about this, he said, giving her a menacing wink, that would be really bad for my image!

Conclusion

Yo, trying to stifle his laughter when he saw the expression of surprise on the attentive Jack's face, turned to the sleeping Samu and pretended to cover her with the blanket.

- Did you like it? asked Odede, also trying to refrain from laughing at Jack'expression.
- It's not exactly the story I had in mind, replied the latter, dumbfounded.

I warned you, said Odede, visibly satisfied with her story.
- He really changed the story, your grandfather.
- Yes, of course.
- And why did he do that?
- Because we can always change our story, however we like, if we don't like it as it is.
- Ok…
- Like yours, for example, your story, you can change it as you wish, if you really want.
- What do you mean?
- That's what my grandfather helped me understand. If you like the story of your life, don't change anything. But if it is not the case, you can rewrite it as you wish, do what you want with it, choose your characters, what you will live with them, the beginning, the unfolding, the end. It is we who create what we live, but too often we live unconsciously, by default, because that is what we have been taught to do. But everything can become as we desire, concluded Odede, standing up.
- And what is your grandfather's magic recipe to make that happen?

She advanced towards him, closed fists stretched forward, palms down, not saying a word, waiting for his reaction. .

- I get to choose?

- Exactly, she replied, that is his recipe.

- What?

- The story of your life takes shape every second by the countless choices you make at every turn.

Jack glanced at Yo, then returned to Odedé.

- Let me explain, she said, kneeling beside him. At any moment, you have the possibility to choose what you will experience. What you feel about what's going on in your life, what you interpret of events that have already happened, each time you feel something, you make a choice, and when you act on it, your life becomes the result of the choice you made. However, you always have the choice to interpret what is happening to you in any way you want, and from there, the choice of actions that you will take... It takes a bit of practice and good will to change your thinking habits, of course, but it is doable.

- And what is the link with the history of the frog?

- In the original story, as you already mentioned, the scorpion stings the frog, explaining that stinging is in its nature and that it could not do otherwise, and they both sink.

- Right!

- Now, in the teachings of my ancestors, my grandfather included, we are shown that we have always had this capacity to be able to change things, if you really want to, of course, no matter what you came to believe to be your nature. You can also manage to transform your nature to be how you want it to be, and transcend it... just like the scorpion. He still stung, but he made the choice to control his nature to be what he wanted it to be, and to control his feelings and his actions to obtain the result he wanted, that is that is to say keep his word and do no harm to the frog, in this case.

- Of course, one must believe that all this is possible.

- What you believe...

- Becomes my reality, said Jack, finishing Odede's sentence... Yes I know!

__Double view__

- It's not raining anymore!

Months had passed and Jack was looking out the window of the office watching the last drops of rain falling from the leaves of the tree outside.

- Stopped a few minutes ago, replied the lady, in business attire. Where were you?
- Lost in my thoughts somewhere...
- Then your thoughts must have been far away, it's been a while since I've seen you silent like that.
- Excuse me, he replied, turning around, I guess don't have much to say today.
- Take your time. Speak when you feel ready.
- Actually, I think this is going to be the last time we meet. To be honest, that's what I was thinking about.

Surprised, the psychologist scrutinized him for a moment before answering:

- No need to make a hasty decision, we can talk about it next week if you want.
- It's all thought out. I have been coming to see you for a few weeks now and my decision has been made. I realize that the problem is not in my head, but in my heart, and for that, you cannot help me.

As soon as his sentence was finished, he placed an envelope on the psychologist's desk, then headed for the exit.

- The payment is in there, including for today's session, he said, opening the door. Then he left feeling unburdened and headed in the direction of the parking lot where his wife was waiting for him.

- I told her I wouldn't be coming back, he said to her once in the car.
- Really? Are you sure of your decision?
- More than certain. I think it did her more good than it did me, said Jack laughing. This morning, I had nothing to say to her and I realized that, unlike other days, everything depended on the state of mind I was in, and that I was completely unaware of it.
- What do you mean?
- That without knowing why, there are times when I feel good and others not. That, without realizing it, I get stuck in this feeling wondering why, without being able to understand. Because, he continued looking her in the eyes, when I think about my life everything is fine, everything is the way I want it, and despite everything...
- What happened to make you realize this?
- Watching the rain fall through the window earlier, I could see the reflection of the office inside and what was happening outside at the same time. That's when things clicked for me.
- That is to say?
- I saw the same world from two different points of view, simultaneously, and I could choose, at my discretion, which one I wanted to focus on.
- I'm not following you...
- My daily life is similar. I can look at my life either with my head or with my heart, what I "intellectualize" if you will, or what I feel. And I realized that I was trying to "intellectualize" what I was feeling... Not a good mix, is it?

Diane remained silent, not knowing what to answer.

- Don't worry, Jack continued, noticing her reaction, I finally understand myself... well, I'm getting there gradually.
- I am happy to hear it, but if you could explain it to me, I'd appreciate it... As much as I'd like to, I still cannot read your mind.

- Very well, he said smiling, here you are: you know me well enough to know that I always thought that logic was the best way to go.

- Yes...

- Even if in recent years, I have changed my way of seeing life a lot and have improved my sense of priorities, I suddenly realized where I was making a mistake.

- ...?

- I always had the feeling that I was missing something.

- Yes, I know, you told me a few times, and you found what it was?

With half a smile, Jack replied:

- Not completely, but I feel that I am on the right track... And I think I also know where to find what I'm missing.

Reality, or...

- We must always be proud of what we are, regardless of what we have done and the results obtained.

Jack was going back to his car after having waited three hours sitting in front of Bruno's tombstone, hoping for some form of communication without anything happening; he kept repeating this sentence to himself as he left the place.

- Where have I heard that before? he wondered when suddenly he thought of Bruno's friend whom he had visited in the hospital.
- Right, he thought. It's me!
- Huh?
- It's me!
- Roby?

Jack stopped walking and turned to look towards the cemetery.

- OK, what's going on there?
- Nothing special, he thought again, as if Roby was talking to him. Do you think there is only one way to communicate with us?
- What I think comes from you? he asked in his head, hoping not to receive an answer.
- Yes, me and many others, he heard himself think. It's simple, wouldn't you agree?
- I don't understand...
- What you believe becomes your reality!
- Bruno?
- At your service...

Jack went to sit on a bench in the nearby park, while wondering about his mental state. But what is happening to me? he wondered. When I was having imaginary discussions with Bruno, that was fine, but now... Roby..!

- When you ask for answers, answered Roby, no matter how you receive them, the important thing is that you receive them, right?
- Maybe, but it all happens in my head, in my imagination...
- Your whole life on Earth is spent in your imagination. What you experience is only the physical manifestation of what you imagined... and believed first.

Jack looked around, admiring the landscape, telling himself that no one and nothing could have suspected what he was going through right now.

- It's always like that, said Bruno's voice. You are the only person in your world, like the billions of other people around you: they too are the only people in their own worlds.
- Forgive me, Bruno, but I thought that what was happening between us was due to the place where I was going to meet you, or to the bond of friendship which united us.
- That too, but you are developing an even more natural way of communicating with a part of yourself, because what you believe to be us at the moment is that invisible part of yourself. Some will call it your *divine part*, others your *soul*, still others your *source*, but the label does not matter. You simply discover its existence by being more and more aware of life. And the more you are aware of your inner, let's call it... divinity, the more you are connected with this dimension of yourself, and it is with this part of you that we are all connected.
- Wow, wait a minute...
- And I would even add, Bruno interrupted, ignoring Jack's reluctance, that it's also like that on Earth, but few people realize it.
- Sorry?
- Do you really believe that the people around you are there by chance?

- Uh...

- Have you ever thought of someone and at the same time that person calls you?

- Yeah...

- Or to think of someone for no reason and to feel the sudden urge to call them to find out that they are not doing very well?

- Uh huh...

- We are all connected, Jack, the difference lies in the fact of whether you are aware of it... or not.

- But I thought to communicate with them... the people who have disappeared, said Jack, hesitating on the words, you had to be meditating or concentrating, or anyways something like that.

- It's however you want, if you think it should be like that, it will be. If you think it's different, it will be too. You live what you believe...

- That's a little too easy, right?

- It is whatever you decide... In your everyday life, when you talk to someone, you look at them and pay attention to what they say, right? As it was for us, in fact.

- Yes, of course.

- But if you walk in the street with this person and pay attention to what is happening around you, like traffic, people you meet, sidewalks, etc. and the person says something to you, can you hear it?

- Uh... yes, well, I think.

- Is it also possible that you can't hear it?

- Yes, if I'm too busy with something else, but just because I didn't hear it doesn't mean I don't know that she spoke to me...

- So you know she talked to you?

- Of course.

- But as you were preoccupied with something else, you did not answer...

- Right.

- Was there really any communication between the two of you?

- Yes... No... Maybe ...

- But you did not have to be focused on the person to know that she had spoken to you, and in fact when you are concentrated again, you will surely ask her to repeat what he said...

- Surely!

- And you will not have to be, still there, super concentrated or to be in a meditative state to hear it, you will only have to be attentive?

- Okay...

- It's like that, Jack, you don't need more than that. You ask a question and, if you are attentive, what you imagine to be the answer is simply the reception of our thoughts, and I say our, because we are all together in this dimension called invisible. In reality, we are one!

Jack looked around, life continued to unfold around him, and then he heard himself say aloud:

- If you believe, and since what we believe becomes our reality...

And while continuing to observe life unfolding around him…

- But let us help you understand ..., he perceived then again ... in thought!

<u>**Never finished**</u>

- What I thought I was missing, in reality, was what I had not yet discovered.

Seated for a picnic on the top of a mountain they had just climbed on a hike, Jack and Diane, the years having passed, discussed their lives while admiring the superb landscape which extended past the horizon.

- It's never over, Jack continued, each time we think we have everything settled, all understood, something happens that leads us to discover another aspect of life, another point of view, another way to understand... and each time I was in this situation, I believed that I had not yet understood, when, in reality, I was on the brink of discovering something new.
- Hence your feeling of not understanding what was going on? asked Diane.
- Exactly! I confused the new with the old.
- And how did you learn to tell the difference?
- Talking to myself, he said with a smile. But if I'm being serious, I would say by trusting myself. By stopping doubts and fears from deceiving me by confronting myself with my own beliefs. It's easy to talk and have great theories about how life works when everything is going well, but when the time comes that everything goes wrong, many people fail to practice what they preach.
- Did that happen to you?

- Yes, it happened to me, and it is perhaps one of the most difficult things to succeed, to continue to believe when things are not going well. It is as if you are faced with the fact that what you believe does not work is because of the difficult thing you are going through. You say to yourself: How did I create this? It does not resemble me! And there you start questioning everything you think you understood, when really it comes from yours yourself, not what you know.

- That is to say?

- Everything comes from you. If you want your life to be a certain way, you must first create it inside you. You have to be quote un-quote, already what you want to experience.

- I don't understand you, how can we already be what we want to become?

- By imagining it, seeing it, feeling it, first.

- Explain...

- Do you like water?

- Yes.

- Do you like scuba diving? Do you like to admire the fish in their environment?

- You know that...

- But to be able to live this, you must prepare yourself, learn what it takes, how your equipment works, learn the rules so that you do not have an accident, go into the water, etc.

- OK, but where are you coming from?

- That to achieve the life we want, if we resume diving, for example, so that you can have the experience you want with the fish, you must be in their world, in the water, already be in the world you want to live in, so that you can achieve what you want in it.

- And what is the link with: everything comes from oneself?

- To live the life you want, it's the same thing. We must there too, internally of course, come to feel as if what we want already exists in our life, or if you will, already be, always internally of course, in the world in which you wish to live," as if it were already accomplished, before it can even happen from a physical, or material point of view... if that makes sense.

- Okay, I understand your point of view and I admit that, even if I have to think about it again, I think it makes sense.

- A small detail...When we have identified and understood the feeling of what we want, we then have to take the actions that we believe are the right ones to achieve what we want, which creates a movement of energy... in connection with what we believe possible, and there, I repeat, what we believe possible, in our lives.

- Is it so important this believing it is possible?

- Yes, because if you don't think it's "possible" for you, it won't be.

Diane took a moment to think, before continuing:

- But you also spoke of *being*, earlier, what did you mean?

- That life is a reflection of what we are and becomes what we are...

- And we become what we believe... said Diane, finishing her husband's sentence. And what was, for you, the best way to achieve this?

- Here and here, said Jack, pointing first to his head and then to his heart. Believe in myself, imagine the life I want with clarity so that I can feel it clearly enough for it to become possible for me. You can take action and do whatever you think is necessary to achieve what you want, but it all starts with you...What you believe, becomes!

Diane was stunned by her husband's speech.

- When I hear you talk like that, it sounds simple.

- It is indeed, perhaps too simple for most of the world surely, but it is necessary all the same, in spite of the apparent simplicity, to do your best to put that into practice on a daily basis. And if you are not too demanding, not too hard on yourself, if you do not judge yourself by the results but rather by what you feel, by what you become as you go measure, it is achievable... gradually.

- Where did you learn all this? she wondered. I may have known you for all these years, and yet I feel as though I'm still discovering you...

- I hear voices in my head, he replied, laughing. But don't worry, it's not dangerous.

- I don't worry, said Diane laughing with him, I trust you completely. I even admit that I really like this new Jack, he's very… inspiring!

Jack looked his wife's eyes, overwhelmed by the love he felt in that moment, and taking her in his arms, he replied:

- Me too, darling... me too!

The END..?
Or then again... maybe not!

Liability Limits

The author, translator and publisher do not claim or warrant the accuracy, applicability and appropriateness or completeness of the content of this product. They decline any responsibility, express or implied, whatever it may be.